All I Feel Is Love

All I Feel Is Love

Published by Gatekeeper Press
7853 Gunn Hwy., Suite 209
Tampa, FL 33626
www.GatekeeperPress.com

ISBN (paperback): 9781662953316

All I Feel Is Love

Lindsay Bomstein, MA

gatekeeper press
Tampa, Florida

"The title points to this being a book about love, which it is, but this love encompasses so much, it feels important to name it all. This is a story about grief and hope and tragedy and wonder. It's about being with the unexpected and wild nature of life and learning to love it fully (or as much as is possible in any given moment). Lindsay shares her heart and wisdom, documenting the mundane moments that unexpectedly shift into core memories and life shaping experiences. This book is a touching memoir of heart and soul with generous guidance for all of us tender-hearted humans navigating similar life events."

Rebecca Luttrell, MA
Psychotherapist, Grief Counselor, and co-host of the
All The Grief Podcast

"Lindsay's words are the smell of something baking in the oven, the blanket, the hot tea, and the hug she suggests we give ourselves."

Katherine Snow Smith
Author of Stepping on the Blender and Other Times Life Gets Messy

Dedicated to my mom and dad.

Author's Note

I believe deeply in sharing our stories, experiences, and truths. For some of us, this comes naturally; for others it may be the work of a lifetime. Maybe you were told to be quiet when you were a kid or that you talked too much or not enough. Maybe you feel your story doesn't matter, or you don't know where to begin, or you fear sounding ungrateful, or it feels too indulgent or uninteresting.

But we all have stories to tell. And the telling is in and of itself healing. We can simply begin right now, at this very moment. How do you feel? How does your body feel? Where do you feel this? What is your heart telling you? Your gut? What are you hungry for? Longing for? Scared of? What do you want? Are there stories from your past yearning to be processed, examined, shared? What have you learned from going through what you went through? Try writing it down without judgment.

When we reckon with our personal and collective histories, there is room for growth and understanding. My story is about growing up and learning how to keep going in the face of profound loss and change. I had to learn to stop looking outside of myself for answers and start loving and trusting myself exactly as I am. Quieting the noise and connecting to my soul has enabled me to stay present in my body while creating more spaciousness in my life.

When we belong to ourselves and feel more grounded in our skin, we allow our pain and joy to inform us and, ultimately, transform us. In turn, when we share these stories, we help others heal too. We belong to each other. And what we say and do matters greatly.

The heart of this book is about the death of my parents. While losing parents is the natural order of things, it doesn't mean it's easy. There have been so many ups and downs, but grief has taught me how to enjoy life more fully and be a more compassionate human being. It's my sincere hope that by sharing my experiences with you, dear reader, you will feel less dread about death, less alone in your grief, and more joy in your living.

Writing my stories has helped me process my experiences and mine for the gold inherent in them. Writing is both a meditative and spiritual practice for me. When I write, I let go, I tune in, I get into my body, and I listen to what wants to come through and what yearns to be expressed. I practice allowing it all and politely telling the critical, judgmental voice to take a hike.

Writing centers and grounds me, helping me to see that I am a small spark in the infinite cosmos, but a spark nonetheless. Writing is hugely therapeutic, and writing as well as sharing my stories through my blog and in circles with family and friends has been profoundly healing.

I hope this book inspires you to write and share your stories too, be it on paper or in communion with others. Your wisdom is exactly what is needed to not only survive but thrive in this crazy, beautiful world.

Part I

*Go find yourself first
so you can also find me.*

— Rumi

Chapter 1

Change

"I don't do well with change," my mom used to say. One of the biggest changes for our family came when I was six and my dad told me, my sister Kerry (age twelve at the time), my brother, Rich (age fourteen), and my sister Heather (age seventeen), with my mom standing close by, that he had accepted a new job with the cosmetic company Revlon after having been let go from his position with Singer. I didn't think much of it. Until he said the job was in Scottsdale, Arizona, where he emphasized that it was sunny all the time. I had no idea where Arizona was, but I could tell by the loud silence in the room that it was kind of a big deal. My mom fought back tears as my dad spun the news as a fun, new adventure.

We lived in Chatham, New Jersey, in a red colonial with a steep driveway that was great for both sledding and biking. My parents, Bill and Sue, were high school sweethearts, and both had stellar smiles. My dad was six-foot-two, and my mom was *maybe* five-foot-two. My mom was a brunette with brown eyes, and my dad, a sandy blond, went gray in his mid-thirties. One of my favorite photos is the two of them sitting cross-legged on my mom's parents' family room floor, beaming. They gave off the vibe that they really liked being around each other and never argued much. They loved their friends and neighbors and going down to the Jersey shore in the summer where we'd spend hours upon hours in the ocean and playing in the sand. My mom would tell everyone within earshot that New Jersey was where she was born and bred, although I always heard it as "born and 'bread.'" She was proud to be from the garden state.

My dad was from Connecticut, lived in Scotland as a wee lad, and moved to New Jersey at age twelve with his mother, Alice, and his two younger brothers, Bob and Doug, after his father, Graham, died from an allergic reaction to penicillin at the age of thirty-seven. It has always made me feel sad that I didn't get to know my grandfathers, as well as grateful to have had the opportunity to spend time with my grandmothers, Alice and Ruth (my mom's mom). My mom's dad, affectionately known as Dick (a tricky name to say the least), died from complications of Parkinson's four months after I was born. Ruth, aka Nana, and my mom's sister, my wonderful and quirky Aunt Joan, lived close by. Leaving them was one of the hardest parts about moving, especially for my mom.

In reality, it was a strange time to be moving for everyone but me. Heather was starting college in Virginia in the fall, and Rich and Kerry would be in tenth and eighth grade respectively, certainly not ideal ages to be the new kid from another state. Family friends threw us going-away parties abundant with alcohol and tearful goodbyes. But as we got closer to leaving, my excitement grew because our new house had a pool in the backyard!

We arrived in Paradise Valley in August as Heather started college and the temperature was well above one hundred degrees. Surprisingly, it was raining that day. My mom said it looked like Mars as it was brown and vastly different from the greenery and manicured lawns in the New Jersey suburbs. There was a wide, expansive sky and succulents that looked like they belonged on the ocean floor. And the mountains! One, Camelback Mountain, looked like a camel lying down.

Our new house had no grass (not an environmentally friendly move—my dad would eventually put in sod and irrigation) but had plenty of pebbles and dirt. When my dad's brother, my Uncle Bob, saw a photograph of our yard for the first time, he referred to it—not incorrectly—as kitty litter. My mom was not thrilled about the desert landscape and missed the water.

It was the summer of *The Karate Kid* and the Cabbage Patch Kids craze. I turned seven a week after we moved and received my very own Cabbage Patch Kid named Melva with tight blond curls and her adoption papers for my birthday. Soon after, only a few days into first grade, I met Kristi—my oldest and to this day one of my very best friends—on the playground while singing a Pop-Tarts commercial. She was shy and friendly, I was anything but shy, and we became fast friends.

I loved going to her house where we'd swim and play on the mountain in her backyard. We'd climb rocks and try to avoid falling on prickly pear cactus. I'd eat all her food, especially the boxes of Crispix cereal, while sitting in her pantry and taking piece after piece of fluorescent-green gum from her overflowing "gum drawer" in the kitchen. At my house, we made up songs and performed elaborate plays and dance routines for my family.

Kristi has always gotten me—and I, her. To this day, there are times when we talk daily and times when weeks go by without a call, yet nothing changes. We're low-maintenance friends and know we are always here for each other.

My elementary school was within walking distance from my house, but my mom drove me to school because she was scared that I would get kidnapped. In her defense, there were a lot of rumors about Snaggletooth, a creepy kidnapper who might be hiding in our pink azalea bushes. My school was very orange and also had a cafeteria/auditorium known as a cafetorium. I was in a number of plays in that cafetorium performing in musicals such as a play about Cabbage Patch Kids, computers, and a Halloween-themed production where I played Happy Medium, a fortune teller who sang a song that went, "I can tell your fortune, I foretell what time will do to you." I don't really appreciate that I remember the lyrics to these absurd songs from forty years ago but can't remember the name of the person I met five minutes ago.

The best part about my dad's job in manufacturing with Revlon was the samples of lipstick and palettes of eyeshadow he would bring home. Kerry and my mom hardly wore makeup, so I ended up with most of it. I'd play "spa" with Borghese mud masks and apricot body scrubs, and I experimented with blue, purple, green, and pink eye shadows with Kristi. I might have looked like I had pink eye on occasion, but it came in handy when I was playing dress-up and wanted to be Madonna and Cindy Lauper.

My dad quickly adjusted to the laid-back lifestyle in the Valley of the Sun. It was harder for my mom as she missed her people terribly. She would often say decades later that she felt she was too hard on my dad during that time. However, I never witnessed this. But my mom tried. She joined the Newcomers Club, played bridge, and began walking with friends. My parents enjoyed gin and tonics poolside in the evenings during sunset and learned how to play golf. They went to Arizona State football games with friends and went to dinner at a restaurant where the piano player would see my mom and start immediately playing "New York, New York" for her. The first few times, she cried.

I quickly acclimated like my dad. I had good friends and spent countless hours outside. The majority of our time as a family was spent swimming in our pool with our golden retriever, Buffy. One of my favorite pastimes was wearing goggles and watching Buffy doing laps underwater. We had a lot of visitors from the northeast, whom my dad enjoyed touring around. Sedona was a favorite with its brilliant red rock and church built on the side of the mountain.

Once, when I was in sixth grade, my dad brought home Debbie Gibson's new perfume, Electric Youth. The pink-and-black bottle with the neon-pink spring was the coolest thing I had ever seen. I brought it to school to show my friends and sprayed some of the rad new scent in art class, which somehow led to it falling on the ground, shattering, spilling everywhere, and inciting utter chaos. Mr. Hogan, the art teacher whom I always liked and even made up a song about, was not thrilled with my unruly behavior, and I ended up getting suspended for a day. Having a dad in the cosmetics industry was a real liability.

My parents were annoyed with the school for suspending me over something as silly as spilling perfume. I remember my mom saying, "It's not like she brought drugs to school." That didn't happen at my elementary school, but it did at the high school my brother went to where there was a story in *Time* magazine before we moved about the copious amounts of cocaine there. My parents were glass-half-full kind of people and always made the best of a situation. And although my mom never felt that she did well with change, we would quickly come to understand that change was truly the only constant.

Chapter 2

Everything Doesn't Happen for a Reason

When I was sixteen, my dad was "let go" from his job with Revlon. I was a sophomore, and my siblings were all back in the northeast having gone to college in Lynchburg and Richmond, Virginia, and Boston. My hardworking father, who wore a jacket and tie every day to work (even when it was 110 degrees in the summer) was now sitting in his makeshift office in my parents' bedroom with the mauve-colored carpet and the stationary bike. I'd spent many a Saturday night in their bedroom while they got ready to go out, watching Star Search with Ed McMahon who I thought looked like my dad.

It made me feel unsettled to know that he was out of work. My mom had been a stay-at-home mom working her ass off to raise four children, pay the bills, and manage a home, including all the cooking and cleaning since having Heather. There was talk of jobs in Minneapolis and Hong Kong, and eventually, a headhunter (a term thankfully not used too much today but one I heard ad nauseam then) found him a job with another cosmetic company back in New Jersey. It was a dream come true for my parents to be heading back to New Jersey, near family and old friends and closer to the water. This time I was the one bummed to move.

I asked my parents if I could stay in Scottsdale to finish my junior and senior year of high school, a plan Kristi and I had concocted and one she had already discussed with her parents. Understandably, my parents were not on board with it. My father made it very clear that we would be moving together as a family, which deep down I understood and accepted.

In February during tenth grade, my dad moved back to New Jersey to start his new job where he lived with my brother. My mom and I finished out the school year and headed to New Jersey the following summer. My dad came back on some weekends, but it was hard on my parents who got married when they were twenty-one. Being the thoughtful and caring parents they were, they did let me stay with my boyfriend (yikes) and Kristi for a couple of weeks before officially moving. Unbeknownst to me at the time, those months in Scottsdale without my dad and ordering takeout taco salads with my mom were preparing us for the not-so-distant future.

The day I arrived in New Jersey, my brother, Rich, picked me up from Newark airport in his white Volkswagen Fox with a Dancing Bears bumper sticker on the back. We shared a love of the Grateful Dead, and I used to think I wanted a tattoo of rainbow-colored bears dancing in a circle around the sun on my ankle or wrist. Thank God that never came to fruition and I opted for a nose ring at twenty-one instead, which could easily disappear.

Rich told me he was going to take the scenic route to our new house, which up until that point I had only seen in pictures. We drove on winding roads with giant trees and silver sage leaves hugging us on either side. The air felt cooler and wetter, a welcome respite from the dry heat of Arizona. We listened to Blind Melon with the windows down and smoked Marlboro Lights.

When we got over a small bridge, now in our new town called Rumson, the sun sparkled on the water, and as much as I didn't want to move, I felt a tinge of excitement about a new beginning. It was satisfying to be near the water after living in the desert for ten years. Smelling the salty Atlantic Ocean air brought back memories of being little and running from the waves while holding my dad's warm hand. I loved to tease my dad when he would stand with his arms crossed, feet stuck in the sand, staring for what felt like hours at the ocean. I always wondered what he was thinking about.

I grew up hearing stories of sailing excursions with his brothers and about docking at a restaurant called Barnacle Bills in Rumson where we would eat hamburgers, throw peanut shells on the floor, and grab chocolate mints on the way out the door. Now we go for the Long Island iced teas, fried zucchini, and mozzarella sticks. There is no more throwing of peanut shells due to the prevalence of peanut allergies and no more mints (also affectionally known as "pee mints" by me and my friends because people would use the bathroom and likely not wash their hands before grabbing a few as they walked out the door).

Pulling into our new driveway and seeing our house for the first time felt promising and gave me butterflies. It was a pretty two-story colonial, and my bedroom was much more spacious than my old one. The backyard was covered in tall trees that would change their colors in the fall and bloom in the spring. And it too had a pool! My dad was over-the-moon excited about this backyard and admittedly chose this particular house because of it.

After I was more or less settled in our new house, I had a few weeks of summer left before junior year officially started. Sally, my other best friend from Scottsdale, who had moved from Phoenix to Minneapolis after eighth grade, came for a visit. We spent the week painting my new bedroom a deep royal blue, going to the beach, and eating ice cream at the local ice cream spot, Crazees.

I wore a lot of tie-dye shirts, jean shorts, and Birkenstocks. My hair was long and straight like Marcia Brady's. The girls in Rumson seemed mostly preppy or sporty and carried Dooney & Bourke purses with ducks on them. I worried about fitting in and finding my people, knowing it was going to be challenging to do so.

School started, and it was as awkward and painful as an '80s after-school special. Lunches were the worst of it as I tried to prove my worth and likeability while sitting at a table that first day with a bunch of girls from my grade. They were nice enough but not overly friendly. I ate my quintessential New Jersey pork-roll-and-cheese sandwich and a chocolate chip cookie. A very healthy meal indeed.

When I sat at my desk in history class, the teacher, a youngish man who resembled a leprechaun, called me Arizona and told the other students to stop being snobby and give Arizona a warm welcome. A few people smiled and said hello. When I met the other new girl, Erica, who had recently moved from Virginia, in the hallway one day, I practically jumped on her. I was so thrilled to not be the only new kid. We became fast friends, and it truly felt like a gift from God that there was another new student in my grade who was friendly and easy to talk to.

I missed my boyfriend and friends in Scottsdale, but by Thanksgiving, Erica and I had become attached at the hip. When her mom and stepdad went to see his daughters for the holiday, it was decided that Erica would spend the holiday with us due to the long car ride and recovery from a recent surgery. The scar was right underneath her butt, and if it wasn't hard enough being new in a small homogenous school where everyone had known one another since the womb, Erica had to stand in class and while eating as she healed.

Before Thanksgiving dinner at my house, we hung out at Erica's and listened to The Smashing Pumpkins while baking apple pies. Erica was a rock star in the kitchen and knew how to make a lot of yummy things, which blew me away since I was clueless when it came to cooking and baking. Back at my house, we had a traditional Thanksgiving meal complete with cranberry sauce out of a can, stuffing, green bean casserole (the kind with cream of mushroom soup and onion crispies on top), turkey, and mashed potatoes—which was my dad's specialty (his trick was using a ricer, lots of half and half, and a gracious amount of butter). Richard and Kerry and my grandmother, my dad's mom, Pom Pom, were also joining us. When my oldest sister, Heather, was a toddler, she coined the name for my dad's mom because Pom Pom often made argyle sweaters, blankets, and hats—some with pom poms on them.

Pom Pom was a Scotch drinker and said wonderfully strange and sometimes embarrassing things like, "Watch your tongue, bud," and "Good night, Nurse!" She was very flexible in the literal sense of the word, and when I think of her, I envision her in a peach terry cloth tracksuit sitting cross-legged on a chair with a cigarette in her right hand. After Thanksgiving dinner, we listened to "I'm Too Sexy" by Right Said Fred as I put a cowboy hat on Pom Pom. We danced, laughed, and ate our pie, which was delicious. It was a great, albeit ridiculous, night—which is my favorite kind.

A week later, Erica and I went shopping at Toys R Us for an upcoming toy drive after school with friends. By the time I got dropped off at home, the sun was already low in the late afternoon sky. The minute I walked through my front door, I sensed something was wrong. The house was dark with no lights on, and the only sound was the low hum of the refrigerator. My mom wasn't there, and she was usually home that time of day sitting on the couch watching the news or in the kitchen unpacking groceries or getting dinner ready. I went into the family room and opened the sliding glass doors to let our golden retriever, Buffy, out. Then I walked into the kitchen to see if there were any messages on our answering machine, but I only found a note on the counter.

Earlier that day, I had a strange sense that something had happened. This awful feeling came over me, causing my stomach to hurt. At the time I was in my anthropology class watching *Harold and Maude* for some reason. That could have had something to do with the uneasiness I felt; it's not exactly a cheery movie.

But in the dark kitchen, when I saw the note written in my mother's hurried handwriting, the sense of unease crept back up my body and stopped abruptly in my chest. The note revealed that my dad had been in a car accident and that she would call me when she could.

I paced and prayed, turned the TV on, then turned it off. I tried to eat, but I couldn't. I went upstairs to my bedroom and sat on my floor. I put on an Enya CD that my dad had recently bought me after picking me up from the airport after a trip to Arizona earlier that fall. He felt bad for me, knowing I was sad after leaving my friends and boyfriend again, so he took me to the record shop to cheer me up. I thought it was the sweetest gesture, and I was grateful for his sensitivity and thoughtfulness. The music was haunting but beautiful and was the perfect companion on that cold, scary night.

I called Heather and then Erica. Kerry was working a new job in Massachusetts, and I didn't know how to reach her. Heather, now married and a mom to two young boys, had months earlier moved to Denver with her family. We spoke briefly, and I told her I would let her know more as soon as I did. When the phone finally rang, I picked it up and heard my brother's shaky voice. He was with my mom and told me that the car accident had happened in White Plains, New York, about two hours from where we lived. My dad was heading to a meeting when a truck barreled into him.

"It's bad," Rich said, fighting back tears.

I was stunned, barely said much, and then we hung up. I sat in silence and then called Heather back. Sensing my disorientation and inability to get in the car and drive two hours away, she ordered a car service to take me to the hospital. Erica kindly offered to come with me.

When we arrived, I went straight to the ICU to see him, and I was shocked by how he looked. His head was bandaged up, and his face was black and blue and swollen. His eyes were closed, and he appeared to be sleeping. I held his hand and found the familiar pad of his thumb where he had an infection when he was little. The skin there was left fleshy and malleable. My favorite thing to do when I was younger was sit in the little home he'd make for me by bending his knees while still in his work pants and black socks with the golden seams on the toes, as he lay on the couch. I'd play with his squishy thumb or play hairdresser and brush his hair with his red, round brush. At the hospital, no one said the word *coma*, but no one said much of anything. When I walked out of his room, I overheard doctors and nurses saying that he most likely didn't know what hit him.

The doctors didn't know the extent of his injuries. There were more questions than answers. It was hard to believe this was happening. They said, if he survived, it would be a long road ahead with major rehabilitation needed. Would he be able to walk? Talk? All we knew was that he had suffered severe head trauma, and all we could do was wait and see. Wait and see. Wait and see.

The hospital was sterile, brightly lit, and smelled of antiseptic. Hours later, more family arrived, including Aunt Joan, my mom's sister, and my sisters, Heather and Kerry. We all stayed at a hotel near the hospital. I had no idea what time it was. It had to have been late, and the hospital was eerily quiet.

When we got up the next morning, stumbling out of our hotel rooms from lack of sleep and worry, we went back to the hospital. The day moved simultaneously at warp speed and as slowly as molasses. We cried, hugged, and took turns being strong and positive, although none of us was feeling particularly so. How could this have happened? We had just moved back for his new job, and my parents were so happy to be close to family and old friends again.

Once I thought I felt his hand squeeze mine in recognition when I sat next to him in the ICU. I had also brought a Buddha from home and placed it next to him. It was one he bought when he was on a business trip in Japan where he told us he had tried soup with a bird floating in it. I was so bothered by this story when he told it to me that I'll never forget it. The doctors talked to us like my dad wasn't there. I felt like he could hear them, and I worried that their uncertainty and negativity were going to startle him or impact his decision to wake up, making him think that there was nothing they could do for him and no chance for his survival. I wished they would be more positive. I knew he wouldn't want to be a burden on us.

The doctors didn't know anything about him or my family, and here we were in this most personal, intimate, vulnerable time of all our lives. My father was hopeful, enthusiastic, and optimistic. He used to say that things happened for a reason. I was having a tough time swallowing that philosophy at the moment. He was so happy to be back with my mom and by the water after ten years in Scottsdale. They wanted to travel. He hoped to get a sailboat and start sailing again. He wanted to go to Colorado and spend time with his young grandsons. There were so many dreams and plans. He had worked hard to put my siblings through college and pay for Heather's wedding, and he looked forward to his retirement someday.

The next day my brother and I drove down to the house in Rumson to pick up clothes and toiletries for my mom. We had no idea how long we would be living out of a suitcase in a hotel waiting for something, and I had no idea how or when I would return to school. While riding in the car, I felt like I was suspended in a bubble, almost in a full-body daze, and like I could look down from somewhere else and see us. We were just one of the many cars crowding the road, going about our business. It was nothing personal. People in the cars around us were living their own lives, many suffering too.

But we were oblivious to the predicaments playing out in all the cars riding in tandem. There was something about this that felt awfully lonely and cruel. There were men and women honking their horns, driving fast and irresponsibly, and I wanted to scream at them all. I felt paralyzed but thankful to be with Rich in his car away from the hospital, away from the dense, permeating feeling of doom. I yearned for a break from the heaviness. This day was different from all others and somehow also remarkably the same.

Do you know how fragile this all is? I wanted to yell.

I wished everyone realized how precious life was and that it could change in an instant, and maybe then they wouldn't drive so fast or be so selfish and reckless.

We arrived at the house, and it felt weird to be there in the middle of a weekday. Kids were at school; adults were working and doing errands. I heard trucks in the distance, brakes squeaking, beeping noises signaling someone going in reverse. Business as usual.

Not soon after we got there, Kerry called and told us to stay put. She said not to rush back to the hospital because he had taken a turn for the worse. My brother and I froze. My stomach flipped, and my hands shook. We were in the back of the family room with photographs of all of us over the years on the windowsill next to the leafy potted plants. We cried and worried out loud and quietly to ourselves. What would we do if something happened to him? How would my mom survive? They despised being apart.

Kerry called back quickly. They tried to revive him, but his heart had stopped. Two days after the accident. He had just turned fifty-four that October. My dad—my kind, warm, gentle, and generous six-foot-two dad—was gone.

Chapter 3

Winter

The morning of my dad's fatal car accident, we had gotten into an argument. We had been in New Jersey for only three months at that point. My throat was sore that morning, and I was looking for a way out of an upcoming voice recital. I told him I couldn't sing as he was getting ready to leave for the day. He didn't want to hear it. I had started taking lessons with a classically trained voice teacher, an older man named Felix, who was kind but stern. He had me sing "One Hand, One Heart" from the musical *West Side Story*, "Memories" from *Cats*, and "Edelweiss" from *The Sound of Music*.

I recorded "Edelweiss" one day for my dad when I first started working with my voice coach as a kind of gift. In kindergarten I sang the same song on a stage in front of the entire school. And while I don't remember this performance one bit, I heard about it a lot from my mom and siblings. She told me that I sang perfectly in tune on that big stage all by myself and that my dad had tears streaming down his face as he watched me.

I loved singing, but as I got to middle school, I didn't like performing at all. Getting onstage in front of people and being subjected to their opinions and judgment left me feeling way too self-conscious and nervous.

When my dad left for work the morning of his accident, we didn't say goodbye. He was upset with me, and I was annoyed with him all over the upcoming voice recital that I didn't want to do. We both left in a huff. I was being difficult not because I was trying to be but because I was sad and felt lost. I was also a teenager, which meant I could be a self-obsessed pain in the ass. I felt like I didn't exactly belong where I was. Thank goodness for friends like Erica and Kristin. But I still wasn't sure where I fit in. I couldn't help but wonder if the accident had been entirely my fault. I thought to myself that if we hadn't argued that morning, if I had never brought up my sore throat or the recital, he wouldn't have been distracted and would have been paying closer attention to the other drivers on the road. How could I have been so selfish? I was plagued with guilt.

But the morning after he died and before I woke up, I was in my bed and miraculously found myself having a conversation with my dad. It felt lucid and real, and I didn't question for a second whether it was or not. We were standing in the driveway, and he was dressed in his navy suit and tie, smiling widely with his warm grin and rosy cheeks. He appeared relaxed and calm, and he told me not to worry. Waving his hand in front of him, he told me none of this was my fault.

"How could it be?" he chuckled.

He told me he loved me unconditionally and that this was part of a greater plan.

"Everything is interconnected, and everything will all eventually be okay. Trust me," he said.

It was so clear, and his words rang true in every part of my body.

I woke up, and sitting in the core of my dread and sorrow was something unexpected, something like awe and thankfulness. It seemed like a miracle, and it was truer and more real than anything else I had experienced. It was as if I had just been given this incredible gift from my dad that erased the awful guilt I had been stuck with since the minute I found out about his accident. It wasn't my fault that he got in a car accident. Of course it wasn't.

And while I intellectually knew this, the experience of seeing him, of getting to talk to him, helped me feel it, embody it, and metabolize it. I was beyond thankful for the message. It felt big. I told my mom and siblings, and they were happy for me. But as grateful as I was for this mysterious message from the other side, the sadness was overpowering, all-consuming, and raw.

If only I had known the previous week that he wouldn't be here the following one . . . But what if I had known? What would I have done differently? Certainly not let a stupid argument get in the way of me hugging and kissing him goodbye, of saying "I love you." I had to get out of bed, use the bathroom, and eat breakfast, but I didn't know how to do anything anymore because everything felt different.

Just take the next step, one thing at a time, I told myself. Feet on floor, walk to door, open door, walk to bathroom, use toilet, wash hands, brush teeth, put in contacts, walk downstairs . . .

It all took a lot of effort and energy. And looking back now, I realize I was in total shock.

The days and weeks after his death were filled with cards, plants, flowers, casseroles, and so many family and friends coming and going. We had a beautiful funeral that a few of my new friends came to and my boyfriend from Scottsdale flew in for. Because of the support, because we moved through it as one entity, and not yet as separate beings feeling our way through our own vast landscape of grief, we got by. Somehow we got by.

Christmas was only three weeks away, which felt impossible and even cruel. My mom's signature Santa Clauses in all shapes and sizes started appearing all over the house, including the one she bought the day of my dad's accident, the one with a kilt and bagpipes, which stood on her windowsill in the kitchen.

My dad had mentioned to my sister Heather one day on the phone that my mom had been getting an early start on decorating for Christmas because she was so excited to have Heather's family there for our first Christmas in our new home. It was such a strange dichotomy that in the midst of all that heaviness were wooden nutcrackers and a miniature village all lit up and sparkly. There was even a wreath on the front door with dried fruit and a velvety burgundy bow.

If my dad were a holiday, he would have been Christmas. He looked like Santa with his red cheeks, white hair, and belly, which didn't quite shake like a bowl full of jelly but could have if prompted. His smile was dozens of twinkly white lights. My siblings were all home again, and my nephews, ages one and two, kept us distracted and laughing. Aunt Joan was also there. We got a big Douglas fir and decorated it, finding bittersweet comfort in the familiarity and tradition of hanging ornaments. Hearing Christmas music stung and made me cry. I couldn't look at pictures or videos of my dad yet.

I wondered who would buy my mom presents now. My dad used to shop for her and would sometimes take me along, asking for my opinion on a pretty silk blouse or a sweater. I loved those outings with him as much as he loved buying her gifts.

One night, in the blur of the aftermath of my dad's death and persistent holiday cheer, Erica and I passed around appetizers and champagne at her parents' Christmas party. A businessman— maybe someone who worked with Erica's stepdad, a man similar in age to my dad—was making small talk and asked me my name, where I was from, and why we had moved. I told him it was for my dad's job, and as soon as the words exited my mouth, I regretted it, knowing what would come next.

"What does your dad do for work?" he asked.

I froze, too stunned to speak. I hadn't said it out loud yet. I stuttered, my heartbeat sped up, I turned red, and I wanted to run away after blurting out that he had just died. There was no eloquent or gentle way of saying it. "Well, we moved here for my dad's job, but now he's dead." I shouldn't have come. I wasn't ready or prepared for that. I felt trapped. I wanted out. I went out the front door, gasped for fresh air, and drove myself home.

Christmas Eve, which had always been my favorite night of the year, inevitably came. While we were watching TV, a toy robot—unwrapped and waiting for my nephew to see in the morning—sat underneath the tree making weird noises totally unprovoked. It drove my Pepsi-drinking, black-ballet-slipper-wearing Aunt Joan crazy, and she was not shy about letting us know it, which made us all laugh.

Even during those darkest days, there was still laughter. And even though so much had changed, there were things that remained the same. Those things like our Christmas ornaments, watching TV together, and eating our favorite meals, like my mom's chicken with wine and grasshopper surprise for dessert, served as anchors keeping us tethered to each other, to our past, and to the ground beneath us.

This is something I remember about this time maybe more than anything. As devastated as we all were, we had each other. It was surprising to me then, and it's surprising to me now that it wasn't all terrible right after my dad died. That there was light and laughter and even joy. My mom kept us moving forward. She simply kept going and made sure we all followed suit.

It was an especially snowy winter that year with lots of days off from school. The weather provided a buffer between me and the outside world. It was the perfect excuse to stay home and sit on the couch with Erica, who would come over and watch movies with me. We would take turns scratching one another's arms and eating peach gummies. I felt safe at home and protected from pity, watchful teachers, and kids who didn't know what to say so said nothing. One of the toughest things about grief is that it can be so very isolating and lonely.

But there was something else too. I was struck by how everything else that didn't matter fell to the wayside. All I cared about was the people I loved. That realization was freeing. So much really didn't matter. I was sad, but the truth, the authenticity of grief, the realness, was liberating and strangely beautiful.

If we could survive this, then maybe we could survive anything, I'd tell myself.

I had worried about something awful happening a lot in my life. It had. And I was still here.

Chapter 4

Knock on Wood

There was something, an essence, about my dad that I could only describe as wonder. It was, and still is, so very special to me. Now. It wasn't then. Then it felt annoying. He would get so excited and enthusiastic about beauty and nature. And excited about little things too like celery in his tuna salad.

"Kids, will ya look at this?" pointing to the stars, the cactus in bloom, the church built on the side of a rock in Sedona.

There was a childlike awe, a deep appreciation, an earnestness, and a twinkle in his eye when he heard crickets at night in our backyard in New Jersey or tended to the red, pink, and yellow hibiscus by our pool in Scottsdale. When I think about this part of his being now, it's one of the things I miss the most. I can imagine how joyful he would be at this stage of life. It makes me smile and breaks my heart all at the same time.

If you were to ask me if I was religious growing up, I'd say no. We were Presbyterian, but I don't really even know what that means. We didn't go to church very often. Two of my siblings weren't baptized. But if you were to ask me if I'm religious now, I'd say I think so. Usually, I say I'm more spiritual than religious, but that response feels kind of lazy, annoying, or cliché and also true.

But since I was a little girl, I was drawn to this idea of something else, of something bigger. I'm not sure when this started, but I'd say around age eight. My longing was solidifed after my dad died. There was a mystery, and there was something

I couldn't put my finger on that intrigued me. But I didn't like rules, authority, or being told what to do. So there was that.

When I was in elementary school I'd go to church with Kristi on occasion. I was curious about the rituals, the exotic scent of incense inside the church, the stained glass, and the prayers and hymns. Once I remember hearing the congregants reciting, "Give us this day our daily bread" in the same cadence, and I was perplexed and mesmerized. If I expressed this to my parents, which I can't remember ever doing exactly, I think they would have been surprised to hear that I didn't know the prayer like it was just something one simply absorbs by osmosis.

Another time I picked up the New Testament to try and read it when I was in middle school and was turned off by the length, language, and my brother's shock at the fact that I was attempting to read the Bible by choice. I was confused by all of it and didn't know what I was doing.

I never felt that religion was part of my life growing up other than on holidays, which were centered around getting the family together to eat, drink, be merry, and most importantly, open presents.

So where did my yearning for spirituality come from?

Partially, I believe it's innate. I believe that at some point in our lives, if it's not part of your family life or community—perhaps when facing illness or loss or when we're bored, discouraged, or disconnected from others—we start asking the big, existential questions, like: Where were we before we got here, and where do we go after we die? What is the soul? And what is God? And if there is a God, why is there so much suffering? Why wars, poverty, disease? What's the point? Our purpose?

When I was a little girl at sleepover parties I didn't sleep at, there were games we'd play, like Ouija and "light as a feather, stiff as a board," where one person would lie on the ground and we would help them levitate by placing our fingertips underneath their body. I liked this weird realm, this liminal space of communing with ghosts and spirits.

I also had an OCD that manifested as compulsive prayer before bed. And it caused me to do weird things like jumping jacks when I was half asleep. If I didn't do them, I'd tell myself, something bad was going to happen. My mom was a self-proclaimed worrywart, and she was also superstitious. The thought of opening up an umbrella in the house and breaking a mirror where I'd then be subjected to seven years of bad luck scared the shit out of me. I always knocked on wood and still do. I never want to "jinx" myself by saying something out loud such as, "It's going to be a beautiful weekend." If it wasn't, it was most definitely because I said it out loud.

I began experimenting with substances in high school before I moved back to New Jersey and liked the feeling a little too much. It was like entering a different world where the colors looked brighter, the music sounded more intense; but I also felt looser, calmer, and more comfortable in my skin.

One night before I moved to New Jersey, with a couple of friends and my boyfriend nearby in their own drug-induced worlds, I stared up at the glistening stars in the black desert sky surrounding a larger lavender mountain that I loved. I felt a very real sense of being in communion with nature and with a greater force outside of me. Something both within and also without communicated that there was a oneness, a unity, an interconnection among all living, breathing beings. It was hard to articulate, but in this moment of stillness and silence, I felt less afraid of moving across the country. Although I didn't want to go, I had a sense, an embodied knowing, that the move would impact me greatly but that it also wasn't about me and that somehow everything would turn out all right.

With my dad's death, I have always, even after all this time, felt a strong bond to him, to his essence, in a very real and poignant way. It's like we get one another. There are no misunderstandings or miscommunications; it's all crystal clear, an open line of communication. Through his death, a kind of spirituality, a different way of looking at the world and life, came alive in me. And for that I am grateful.

Chapter 5

The Story I Never Wanted to Tell

I was seventeen. I had broken up with my boyfriend from Scottsdale in the late winter over the phone one day as I sat on my bedroom floor, my stomach in knots. Our situation felt hopeless. We had been together since the end of my freshman year and were incredibly close. I adored him. But thousands of miles between us and the intensity of losing my dad caused us to drift apart.

He was graduating from high school in a few months, and I had another year of high school left. We were so young, and staying together seemed inconceivable. I couldn't envision a future that included him moving to New Jersey and working a random job or going to a local community college. We were both distraught, and he wouldn't talk to me on the phone after that. I had imagined that we could ease into separating and stay friends, but it didn't work out that way.

Not much time had passed before I started dating someone else. I didn't want to be alone. And being with my new boyfriend, whether we were taking a walk in the cold or hanging out talking and listening to music, was a nice distraction from the pain and the overwhelming and compounding losses I felt.

I had lost my dad, some of my old friends, my boyfriend, my old life, partially my mom, and my childhood. I had lost so much of myself and who I knew myself to be in such a short span of time that I felt lost and sometimes like I was completely outside of my body.

My dad had been gone for eight months. And now my period was a day late. That was when the sinking feeling started. There was an acidic burn in my throat, and my churning stomach signaled to me that I might be in danger. Flee! Run! Hide! Disappear! I wanted to be little again. I yearned for the intensity of the past year to stop coming in such insurmountable waves, determined, it seemed, to take me down.

If I was pregnant, what would I do? What would happen to me? What if my mom found out?

Maybe the butterflies in my stomach were making me late. Stress can do that, I thought. *I had never been late before. Maybe my period would still come.*

I would check for a few days, imagining wetness in my underwear, only to go to the bathroom and see nothing.

One morning when my mom was out doing errands, I drove to the closest pharmacy, praying not to see any nosy neighbors or parents of friends of mine. I walked through the aisles, bought the first pregnancy test I found, drove home, and ran up the burgundy-carpeted stairs that were installed the day of my dad's car accident. Carpet he never saw.

I went straight into the cold pea-green bathroom. It was quiet. The summer sun was dancing through the windows. It was a beach day outside, a day to be carefree, to feel the warmth of the sun roasting my skin like a rotisserie chicken. But the beauty just made me feel more bleakness, more sorrow. Instead of the beach, I'd most likely be going to the drab, brown building with the blue sign by the railroad tracks next to the Dunkin' Donuts where angry people stood outside holding signs of bloody fetuses.

I carefully unwrapped the test, put the wrapping in a wad of toilet paper, and put it in a paper bag that I would later throw out in a garbage can outside of the house. I peed on the stick and set it on the counter. I waited. Paced. Could hardly breathe. I might get sick. Then I saw it. There it was, as clear as day, the truth of what I was afraid of, what I had been avoiding. Now I knew. The lines indicated that I was pregnant.

I loved babies. I babysat. I was an aunt to my two nephews who lived in Denver. I knew I wanted to be a mom. More than anything else. Someday. But not at seventeen. I was alone. No one was home. I was scared, paralyzed, shaky, in disbelief.

I called Planned Parenthood while I sat on the edge of my mom's bed. No one had to know. I'd call them and ask them what to do. My hands were betraying me; they weren't working. They were so shaky that I had a tough time dialing the numbers. I was struggling with the right words, with talking, with breathing, with making any sense at all. My mouth was dry, and my face felt flushed.

I looked at my mom's shiny dresser, the photos in frames of my sisters, my brother, and me. One of my nephews. Oil of Olay, Chanel No. 5, jewelry. On the wall, a painting of my dad when he was a little boy. Blue eyes, blue shirt, blue suspenders. Where was he now? I was frightened of this painting when I was little because when I moved, his eyes seemed to follow me around the room.

A scary thought pushed through the fog of nostalgia and distraction into the forefront of everything I was thinking and feeling. It whispered that if life was going to be this difficult, how much more could I take? I had a boyfriend, yes. But he was out of town, and I couldn't get in touch with him. We were both in our own wildernesses literally and figuratively at the time. He was camping out West. I couldn't write and tell him that I was pregnant in a letter. There was no email then, no cell phones. That would have been unfair to him to tell him in a letter. But this was unfair to me. I was dealing with this situation by myself when in reality it was the consequence of our actions together, not me alone.

Life is unfair, I thought. God, I hate when people say that.

I still had a tough time believing that my dad was permanently gone and not just on a business trip. The finality was grim. Even after eight months, I frequently caught myself thinking, *Maybe he will reappear. Maybe he is in the witness protection program. Maybe that man driving with the gray hair in the car next to me was actually him.*

I knew it was preposterous, but I couldn't help but think that there must have been a mistake somehow. I had survived my junior year at a new high school. Seismic transitions, major losses, and some good times too. I had made new friends, and I cared deeply for my new boyfriend. I couldn't tell my mom I was pregnant, however. I would not do that to her. Even if we hadn't just moved, even if my dad hadn't just died, I'm not sure I would have told her. We didn't talk about the hard stuff. We didn't talk about sex. We didn't talk about feelings. We skimmed the surface. Sometimes we argued. It's just how our relationship was then. She was there but often felt far away.

I called Erica and told her I was pregnant. I asked her to come over and go with me to Planned Parenthood. What would I have done without Erica? I needed to see a nurse, confirm the pregnancy, and find out when I could do something about it. Erica came over right away, picking me up in her clean silver Saturn. Her car was comforting and familiar, protective like it was keeping me safe. Keeping me from having to deal with the next step, from having something else taken away from me.

The nurse I saw said I'd have to come back for the next clinic. The word *clinic* struck me as odd and cold. She was nice enough but removed. I could tell she had packed up her emotions, picked them up, molded them into a big ball of putty, and then placed them into a box somewhere in a closet or under a bed.

Now what? I'd carry on with my summer plans? I'd pretend everything was normal for a little while longer? But nothing was normal anymore. Still, I trudged on as if it were.

I went on Outward Bound pregnant. I spent weeks in Maine canoeing, hiking, climbing mountains, and sleeping in a tent whether it was raining buckets or hot and buggy. When I climbed a mountain, I rappelled down while breathing heavily and scraping my knuckles till they bled. I hiked with a heavy pack with pots and pans clanking around, all the while panting until reaching our resting place. I was tired, exhausted at times, but I told myself it was all that fresh air that made me feel so sleepy. I was in such denial and so scared to be in my body. I told one girl from Martha's Vineyard what was going on, but she didn't say much. She hugged me though, and that was exactly what I needed at that point.

As far as I know, she never told another soul. I spent one night alone under a tarp on the cold, damp, leafy, and bumpy wooded ground. I wasn't supposed to have a book with me while on my solo in the woods; only a journal was allowed. But I had snuck in *The Shell Seekers* by Rosamunde Pilcher. My mom had told me that was the favorite book of her mom, my Nana, who died when I was in middle school. I used to love sitting next to Nana on the couch and watching her wrinkled thumbs and index fingers rub the arms of her glasses. I needed to feel near her and lose myself in the soft words and family drama that wasn't mine. I needed an escape from my escape. Nana had died when I was in eighth grade, and I missed her.

I wore a whistle around my neck that I was instructed to blow if anything went wrong. I survived the solo and the remainder of my two weeks in the woods. When I got home, I was starving for a hamburger, a long and hot shower, and my bed. My hair was knotty, and my skin was deeply tanned from the sun. I was still pregnant.

I told my boyfriend about the pregnancy while sitting on a bench across from an ice cream shop when we were both home from our simultaneous outdoor adventures. I watched little kids with parents and young babysitters licking the tops off of their dripping ice cream cones so they wouldn't topple onto the concrete or melt all over their sweet faces. It reminded me of my dad and how he would ask for a bite of my dessert and then proceed to eat at least half of it. It annoyed me so much, but what I would have given in that moment to turn back time and "share" a piece of cake or ice cream with him. I fought the urge to get up, run over there, get an ice cream, and pretend I was five again with my parents both physically and emotionally present.

My boyfriend was shocked and sad at the news. He felt guilty. He said all the right things. It was not his fault. It wasn't my fault either. We were casual. Mostly we weren't. But we were that time. We cried together. Some mistakes are so damn permanent.

"Now what?" I told him.

He agreed. He would take me to the clinic in a few days. And then, after the procedure, he would bring me home where I'd lie on the couch and lie to my mom telling her I had bad menstrual cramps.

Decades later, when I'm filling out paperwork at the doctor and they ask me how many times I've been pregnant, and how many living children I have, I wince. And then I feel beyond grateful and fortunate for my three children and for having had an actual choice in the matter—a right we're unbelievably still having to fight for—when I was heartbroken and only seventeen.

Chapter 6

Bears in the Adirondacks

The summer before college, I went camping in the Adirondacks in Upstate New York with Kristin and Erica. Sitting around the fire after dinner, we smoked a joint in our flannels and sweatshirts with my knees pulled up to my chest under my shirt, making me look like I had huge, problematic boobs. I turned to look at Kristin's cute doll face when I saw a bear next to her looking at me. I screamed as we all flew out of our seats and ran toward the lake—all flailing arms and legs. We jumped into our canoe with our pounding hearts and grabbed the paddles to escape the bear and our impending and violent demise. As I got into the canoe, my glasses fell off into the water, and without my glasses (or contacts), I could see about three feet in front of me.

We paddled out into the middle of the lake and tried to calm down. Laughter soon erupted like fizzy water bubbles as we realized how ridiculous we must've looked. We laughed even harder thinking about the seasoned campers around the lake more used to bears than we were. Also, we were high. But looking up at the sky, although blurry, my astigmatism and bad vision couldn't dim the radiance and multitude of twinkly stars above and below us. As my fingertips grazed the glasslike surface of the water, I was mesmerized by the reflection of all those sparkling stars. I felt grateful to the bear for getting us up and out there on the water. If it hadn't been for him, we wouldn't have seen all that spellbinding light.

As we paddled around, looking to return to our campsite, we yelled to the other campers around the lake, "Bear, there's a bear!" In the perfect and still darkness, we spotted a small shining light in the distance. We paddled over, hoping it was actually our site. It was hard to figure out which one was ours because it was pitch-black at all the campsites except for this one little shining light. When we got closer, we saw it was, in fact, a light at our site. We got out of the canoe and made sure the bear was no longer present among our backpacks and tent.

There on the ground was the source of light—a flashlight that one of us must have dropped, although no one remembered doing so. Thankfully and somewhat magically, it was on. We gathered up our stuff, deciding to sleep in Kristin's red Chevrolet Cavalier instead of the ground in the middle of the wild. We were willing to sacrifice crimped necks and stiff legs to avoid being eaten by a bear. Laughing all the way back to the car, we wondered about the flashlight. Maybe the bear turned it on for us.

Or maybe, I thought to myself, *it was my dad.*

I thanked him silently, kissing my fingers and sending them upward, all the while missing him terribly but feeling deeply grateful to have an angel up there in that sea of stars.

When we woke up and headed back to the campsite the next day to pack up our stuff, I went over to the edge of the water and spotted my glasses. I thanked my lucky stars again, grateful to be able to see clearly.

The days after my dad died and before his funeral when cousins, uncles, aunts, and family friends were everywhere, a few things happened that made life after death seem like a very real possibility.

Once, while sitting at the kitchen table, my Uncle Doug's chair broke right underneath him, sending him crashing to the floor. He wasn't some really large guy; in fact, there were far larger there who did not break the chairs. Thankfully, he wasn't hurt, but in typical brotherly fashion, my Uncle Bob chimed in, his laugh audible above the gasps, and shouted, "Gotcha last," a common uttertance between my dad and his brothers.

Another day a glass on a shelf in the dining room appeared to have been pushed by an invisible hand. I watched as it slid to the edge of the shelf and then broke, glass shattering like crackling ice into a million reflective pieces. These inexplicable occurrences and the visitation from my dad the day after he died made me believe there was something else, something more.

And the puzzling but soothing realization that came to me was that our relationships survive death. We keep loving one another long after we die. I feel my dad's love raining down on me, especially when I am in nature. I feel like he has exploded into all these minuscule particles around me. Just like those shards of glass on the floor and the stars we saw when camping. He appears in different ways, in various forms. Maybe he was the hawk sitting on a branch staring at my mom through her kitchen window every December. Sometimes I feel his presence in a cardinal or in the sand dollars that my mom used to find sprinkled on the beach. He is in my brother's, nephews', and son's eyes and smiles and maybe even in that bear that helped us find our way back in the dark. When I talk to my dad now, even though I can't hear him, I know what he will say. I love feeling that we are still connected and maybe even understand each other in a more profound, deeper way.

When I learned about Einstein's theory of energy—that it can neither be created nor destroyed, only transformed—it made me question: what happens to our energy after we die? My dad's energy didn't just disappear; it is still here. It is somewhere and everywhere all at once. We're all made from stardust after all.

Chapter 7

College

When I got to college, I was ambivalent about the whole thing. Amherst, Massachusetts, was beautiful with its deep woods, trickling streams, mountains, and farms. I also appreciated the fact that it was only a four-hour drive from home. I didn't want to be too far from my mom and brother, who had ended up staying home after the past two years of upheaval. My boyfriend was going to UMass too.

While going to college with my boyfriend seemed like a fine idea at the time, in retrospect, it wasn't. We both desperately needed time and space to grow as individuals independent of one another. He wanted to hang with his friends, listen to Phish, and play video games. I was desperate for his attention and affection. The closeness I was seeking was connection with myself, but I didn't know that yet.

I felt like there was an unease bubbling up to the surface in me that was getting harder to ignore. I chalked it up to being homesick. I missed my dad, mom, and brother, the comfort of home, and our new golden retriever, Lucy. I felt exposed, vulnerable, and lonely. And then I felt ashamed for having these feelings. I got along with my roommate, who was goth and quiet and friendly enough. My classes were mostly huge lectures where it was impossible to get to know the instructor. Once again, I felt lost.

I was experiencing social anxiety and still grieving, but I couldn't articulate that, so I avoided it all. I avoided big groups of people, parties, teachers, and my feelings. I was nervous to speak up in class and nervous to be around certain people for no real reason that I could ascertain. It wasn't that I wasn't having fun because I was. I had made a number of new friends, but I was often stuck in my overactive mind to be fully present.

Sometimes I think it's the aftermath of our lives being torn apart that's the hardest. When you're in it, you're in it; you're distracted, busy. Maybe people are checking up on you. There's stuff to do. But when the dust settles, it can be completely overwhelming to figure out where to begin again.

I hadn't processed all of the small losses or the big losses and all the feelings that accompanied them. Sadness as well as grief don't get better or disappear by simply ignoring their existence. I didn't possess the tools to manage my emotions or know how to handle my disturbing and sometimes obtrusive thoughts. I hadn't learned how to regulate my nervous system. I didn't even know what a nervous system was. It was messy inside of me, so I lived outside of my body, looking for comfort and guidance anywhere but within. I didn't feel like I belonged to myself and therefore felt like I didn't belong anywhere.

Before I learned the term *highly sensitive* or familiarized myself with the symptoms of anxiety, before I went to therapy and actually stuck with it, and before I took an antidepressant to help ease my anxiety and the depressive symptoms associated with it, I escaped my big feelings, brushed them under the rug, and told myself I was fine. I put on a happy face. I was jovial, silly, and fun. I distracted myself with pot, alcohol, and my boyfriend. I also told myself that there were many people who had it worse and that I should be grateful, not wallow in my sadness, and not complain. I told myself I was lucky that it wasn't both of my parents or a sibling that had died.

As a child, I often felt different. I was highly emotional and had an undiagnosed OCD. I was terrified of something bad happening. I had a very loving family and a wonderful childhood, and I knew how fortunate I was to have had those ingredients present in my life. But being a human isn't easy.

I had to do something therapeutic, so I signed up for a yoga class. It helped me get into my body and out of my head. I had danced most of my childhood, and it felt good to move and engage my body's strength and flexibility again. The practice of yoga taught me how to breathe properly and piqued my interest about the mind-body connection.

I searched for healers who could help calm my frazzled nervous system and found an energy healer in the phone book. Receiving energy healing from her was relaxing, and working with her was the beginning of a long path of studying different mind-body modalities.

I also attempted to meditate, but when I sat down to do so, without a teacher and not knowing what I was doing exactly (there wasn't YouTube or Google yet, but I had read a couple of books on the subject), I'd feel completely unnerved and overwhelmed by my incessant thinking. I hadn't learned yet that meditation didn't mean not thinking. I hadn't learned yet that we are not our thoughts but are the awareness who notices them. It made me feel antsy and more anxious, so I incorrectly assumed seated meditation wasn't meant for me.

I was experiencing a kind of cognitive dissonance. Part of me wanted to party; part of me wanted to volunteer at a home for adults with mental illness (which I did). I enjoyed feeling helpful and I was good at it at a time when I didn't feel good at much. Part of me wanted to study, and part of me wanted to numb out and take a nap. Another part of me wanted to hide out with my boyfriend. I wanted to remain a teenager, and I also wanted to be an adult. I started college still grieving. And while it was fun and wild at times, it was also challenging and lonely.

My boyfriend and I broke up one afternoon on the grassy hill next to our dorm. We were heartbroken, and we had been through a lot of tough stuff together. I had signed up to travel around the world on a boat with six hundred kids the following fall and felt that I needed a clean start. We both needed it. What started off as a primary feeling of ambivalence when I started college at nineteen was slowly shifting to a twinge of possibility at age twenty-one. And although I still had a lot more work to do—to learn, to grieve, to accept and love all of me—I at least felt I was on the right path.

Chapter 8

I Believe in Miracles

I believe in miracles and serendipity. There are just some things that can't be explained and that I love.

Since the day Kristi and I met on the playground on a piece of equipment that we lovingly referred to as Swiss cheese because it was yellow with lots of holes, we've been connected in a very deep, close way.

Kristi and Sally, my best and longest friends from elementary school, both ended up at University of Colorado in Boulder for college. I tried to visit them at least once a year while also seeing Heather and her family in Denver.

One day Krisiti and I were talking on the phone when she mentioned that she knew of someone going on the same study abroad program I would be attending that coming fall of my junior year of college. She hadn't actually met him, but she had "a feeling."

At one point in the conversation, she said, "I don't know what it is, but I feel like you two are going to hit it off."

She said we both liked the Grateful Dead and took echinacea to ward off colds, which made me laugh. I ignored her enthusiasm and conviction and told her I was done with dating after a tough breakup with my boyfriend of four years. But I couldn't ignore the slightest tickle of butterfly wings flapping against my rib cage when she mentioned this mystery man.

Sally was also going on Semester at Sea. We hadn't lived in the same place since middle school, and I was beside myself with excitement to hang out with her for the semester. I was desperate to spread my wings, experience adventures and different cultures, and meet new people in places like Japan, India, Greece, Spain, and Egypt. I had never traveled abroad before and did not want to be preoccupied with a boy. I didn't want anything or anyone weighing me down. I was desperate to be single and free. Three months on board a cruise ship with six hundred other students taking classes like world music, Indian history, Indian voice, and medicinal plants and herbs all while visiting ten different countries in Southeast Asia, Europe, and North Africa—was an absolutely surreal and incredible dream come true.

Sally and I boarded the ship in the beautiful city of Vancouver, British Columbia, that September with my new hair, which I cut into a bob, and my nose ring, which I got one night in New Jersey over the summer with Erica. Erica opted for a tattoo on her lower back, and when she showed her mom her "tree," her mom exclaimed, "That's not a tree, that's a fucking forest."

Getting on that ship with Sal, I felt like I was nine all over again. I couldn't contain my excitement. It was like I was at a birthday party, and we were about to crush an entire cake after eating Pixy Stix and dancing to INXS and George Michael. My mom and Rich were both there to get me settled, see my cabin, and then take off with Sally's parents before Sally and I, along with our shipmates, spent the next two weeks cruising the Pacific Ocean heading toward Kobe, Japan.

The woman checking me in, an alum of the program, looked at me while holding a clipboard and said smiling, "I met my husband on this ship."

I laughed nervously and politely while my heart did somersaults. Then I looked at Rich and my mom as if to say, *Does she tell everyone this?*

Once on board, I glanced at the wall of students' passport photos in the student union and noticed one belonging to a boy named Josh from Clearwater, Florida. I knew he was the guy Kristi had mentioned.

Uh-oh, he's cute, I remember thinking. Like really cute with freckles, long brown hair, and green eyes.

When I met him a few days later one night at "swell time" (the aptly named happy hour on the boat), he was talking to Sally and was even cuter in person. His freckles made him look like an earnest little boy on the front of a cereal box. If he had just been handsome, it would have been easier for me to ignore him, but he was adorable, and that made it impossible. He was about my height with broad shoulders and oozed warmth and kindness. His hair, which was long, straight, and less windblown in person than in his passport photo, was tied back in a knot. My cheeks flushed instantaneously, and butterflies darted around in my stomach again.

We talked for hours that night and eventually moved our conversation outside to the back deck. There, underneath a moon that appeared to be bobbing due to the rocking of the boat, we laughed effortlessly before our conversation went pretty deep pretty fast. He struck me right off the bat as one of the most charming, most genuine, and brightest people I had ever met. He listened and asked me questions. We had both been through some difficult things, and it was clear from the get-go that we both had scars and maybe still some wounds. But Kristi was right. I should have known she would be because we have a long history of her being right. Turned out we had a lot more shared interests than just the Grateful Dead and echinacea.

A couple of days later, along with another guy named Josh and two guitars, the three of us made a sorry attempt to "play music" together. I use the term *play music* loosely as I'm not sure me banging on a drum while they strummed their guitars constituted playing music. If I could be good at anything, it would be playing an instrument well. But I never possessed the patience or the skill. I stopped piano as soon as I started, and guitar was no better. But thanks to my friend and next-door neighbor, Chip, in my dorm at UMass, I knew how to hold a drum and keep a rhythm going. My sister Kerry, always the generous and thoughtful gift-giver, had given me a conga drum one Christmas, and I loved playing it. It allowed me the feeling of getting in the flow of something, of losing myself a bit. My brain would take a break from my tendency to overthink while my heart led the way.

I took off the sapphire ring my dad had given me for my sixteenth birthday and placed it on a table next to me so I wouldn't hurt my finger or the drum when I played. Sounding fairly awful, we stopped quickly and went to see what else was happening on the ship. When I realized hours later that I had left my ring in the classroom where we held our jam session, I went back to retrieve it. After crawling around on the floor, asking anyone and everyone that I saw if they had seen it, and looking in the Lost and Found, I resigned myself to the fact that it was gone. I was so frustrated and disappointed in myself because I was always losing things. But that ring wasn't just a thing—it was one of the last gifts my dad had given me before he died.

I convinced myself that maybe it was a sacrifice to the gods for being there, for having the good fortune of being on the ship. It was like I was bargaining with the powers that be, something I had done before. *Okay, you can have this ring if I can go on this amazing trip of a lifetime and not have anything too terrible happen.*

The next day I found a note taped to the door of my cabin. I unwrapped it, and in the most beautiful handwriting were the words, "I know this doesn't replace the ring you lost, but I hope it brings a smile to your face." Attached to the note was a little metal smiley face ring from a vending machine. I put it on, and it brought tears to my eyes. It was from Josh. It was such a thoughtful gesture and the first inkling that my ban on dating was over.

I couldn't help but wonder if my dad had something to do with our meeting. My dad had always adored Kristi and Sally. *Maybe,* I think to myself, *he had somehow enlisted their help to make this magic happen.*

I flash back to the night when I first met Josh and the spark of familiarity I saw in his jade-colored eyes. I couldn't help but wonder if the ring he gave me was a sign of things to come.

We kissed for the first time the night before we arrived in China.

A few days later, while hiking on Lantau Island in Hong Kong, we talked to a guy about our age who asked Josh, "Is she your girlfriend?" while pointing at me.

I said back, "If he's lucky."

Then while waiting for the bus, we spotted a sign that read, "Fate might be true, it all depends on you."

If I didn't believe in magic and miracles before, I absolutely did then. And although I was far from home, I felt like I was home. Not home in New Jersey but home in my body. I felt giddy a lot then, like my soul couldn't contain itself and wanted to burst out of my skin and eyes. I felt more like myself than I had in a long time. Like my silly, singing, dressing-up-in-costumes, goofy, funny, and not-so-preoccupied-about-bad-things-happening self.

The places we visited, the music I heard, the people I talked to both on and off the ship—I felt a sense of belonging in all of it. It didn't matter that we didn't speak the same language; we still communicated. Somehow this reminded me of death. We can't communicate in the way we are used to, but communication is still possible. It's just different and maybe even more pure.

It's not that it was all easy. There were many times I felt out of place, on the spot, or totally ridiculous like when I was in China and danced like a chicken to convey to the waiter that I wanted chicken instead of beef. Traveling can be humiliating, and frustrating too. But mostly, I was ecstatic to be on the boat and traveling to all these amazing countries. It was a feeling, and not a place, that showed me where I belonged.

When the trip came to an end, I was heartbroken to say goodbye to Sally, the new friends I met, and the wonderful teachers I had. Saying goodbye to Josh was awful, and I had no idea at that point when I would see him again. Thankfully, he ended up coming to New Jersey to visit me at my mom's house on New Year's Eve, only a week after I got home.

I made the decision not to go back to UMass in the spring. I wanted to hit pause and take inventory of all that I had learned from my semester away and all that I was processing. I needed time and space to plot my next move ao I stayed home with my mom and brother which felt like exaclty where I needed to be at the time.

Chapter 9

California Dreamin'

While I started back up as a full-time student at Antioch University, a small liberal arts college in downtown Santa Barbara, Josh got his first job selling apples at the farmers' market. It wasn't a bad gig and paid surprisingly well, not to mention included the extra perk of delicious fresh apples.

Our first tiny, one-bedroom upstairs apartment, without a dishwasher and washer and dryer was one of my favorite places I've ever lived. The pink carpet was stained with sticky, dark tar that we'd bring home with us on our feet from the incredibly oily beaches. My Great-Aunt Billie referred to our apartment as a hovel once when visiting, and she wasn't incorrect. Our next-door neighbors hung their big, black garbage bags out of their windows, and raccoons raced around, having raves, on the steps outside our front door. But on our balcony where we hosted some raucous gatherings, palm trees swayed in the courtyard with the mountains in the distance. A few times a year, the mountains were snowcapped, appearing in the morning as if an angel had sprinkled some magic fairy sugar dust while we lay sleeping. In our bedroom, the odd, high windows served as a perfect frame for the moon when it was full, white, and pearly.

The sunshine was as intoxicating as the white gorgeous Mediterranean buildings with red-tiled roofs. I was entranced by the purple and red bougainvillea spilling out onto the sidewalks and the novelty of being able to walk to school and downtown. Being at the farmers' markets—abundant in fresh produce and the most colorful, unusual flowers like tuberoses, sweet-smelling freesia, and purple artichoke blossoms—was my favorite way to spend a Saturday morning. There, I'd feel awash in the best part of humanity as someone played guitar and someone else made balloon animals for kids.

I loved the food in Santa Barbara too, especially the taquerias with delicious tacos and horchata, a milky, cinnamon drink that tastes like dessert. I had my favorite coffee spot where I'd enjoy my favorite chai. The Santa Barbara Bowl was close too where we got to see some awesome live music like Beck and Jack Johnson. I adored the friends and personal connections we made, the easygoing vibe, the green gumdrop mountains, and the frolicking sea. I tried to surf on occasion, inhaling large amounts of water up my nose while Josh looked as graceful and elegant as a ballet dancer catching waves on his longboard.

The place captivated me and nurtured me in a way that no other place ever had. It was soothing to my soul to live in that kind of beauty with such stunning nature nearby. Santa Barbara offered me an invitation to rest, relax, and let my guard down a little. It was like my nervous system finally felt regulated for the first time in a long time. And thanks to a few outstanding teachers and special students turned friends from Antioch, it was where I began to gain perspective on the importance of listening, honoring, accepting, and loving myself truly and completely.

During our time there, Josh worked a plethora of jobs and eventually landed in textbook sales. I babysat while finishing my undergraduate degree, sold flowers at outdoor shops where I once had to watch my disgruntled boss kill a mouse with a shovel, and then moved on to sales with a student travel company. When they closed our office and offered us all a job in Portland, Oregon, I declined, and after Josh and I traveled for a few months in Mexico, we headed back to Santa Barbara, where I took a job at a mentoring program with the Council of Alcohol and Drug Abuse and Josh continued his job in textbook sales.

Seven years after we first moved to Santa Barbara, we got married on a beautiful sunny November day. We traipsed across the street from the beach to take photos in the gorgoeus golden presunset light before we signed the ketubah, the Jewish marriage license. The rabbi was at least thirty minutes late, but I wasn't fretting about it...yet. Back from our photo session, Josh's college friend from Emory, Dan, was able to get our rabbi on the phone to find out where the heck he was.

While I hadn't quite gotten around to converting (and still haven't twenty-six years later), I was very proud to introduce our rabbi to my in-laws. They would love him! He was warm and witty and wonderful! And this would make them love me even more! There were about twenty-five family members and close friends hanging around with us in a room at the hotel awaiting his arrival while the rest of the guests stood sipping champagne and lemonade on the lawn. The plan was for our guests to watch the sunset over the Pacific while we signed the ketubah, and then we would tie the knot under the chuppah right after the sun dipped down into the sea.

When Dan, truly one of the nicest guys on the planet, along with his wife, Sarah (also a friend of Josh's from college), and still two of our dearest friends finally got the rabbi on the phone, Dan's face drained of all color, and his mouth hung open as it grazed the floor.

I grabbed the phone from him and said frantically, "Rabbi, where are you?"

"Lindsay," he said, "I blew it."

What in the world does that mean? I screamed silently to myself.

Turns out, he forgot. He could be there, he told me, but he needed to shower and get dressed and it would be roughly another forty-five minutes. I wondered why he had to shower. Had he been playing football? I told him to get there as soon as he could.

At that point, what choice was left but to open the bar and let everyone drink to their hearts' content? My dad's two brothers, in kilts (a nod to our heritage and their days living in Scotland when they were little boys) and yarmulkes on their heads, told everyone that the rabbi was running late but to enjoy themselves while they waited.

By the time I finally walked down the aisle with my Uncle Bob, my dad's younger brother, it was no longer the afterglow of the sunset that we had dreamed of but rather the dark of the night. I was no longer nervous; I was tipsy. Everyone seemed to be. There were candles lit and twinkly lights, and when our rabbi mispronounced our last name, I corrected him and might have silently said, "Fuck." I certainly wouldn't be winning any awards for the best Jewish wedding planned by a shiksa.

But after the collective and silent *oy veys* and OMGs, our rabbi said that while he was disappointed about being late, he was also grateful it was us because he knew we would understand and be kind about it. We laughed, took deep breaths, and kept going. We got married under the chuppah below the stars, and it was the most magical and memorable night of my life. Unsurprisingly, it was also messy and didn't go quite as planned. Isn't that often the way?

I was marrying Josh, the love of my life, and to top it all off, my family and friends from all the different chapters of my childhood and early adulthood came together for this one weekend and surrounded us in what felt like a magical bubble in a gorgeous spot that had been our home for the past seven years. It was perfect, and it wasn't. My dad wasn't there.

A day after our wedding, we left for our honeymoon to beautiful Kauai and Maui for a week. We had previously stayed in hostels in Mexico where we were scared to put our feet on the floor in the showers for fear of getting a fungus. And we camped around the United States sleeping in tents. But on our honeymoon, we stayed in nice hotels where they greeted us with colorful, sweet-smelling leis of gardenias and plumeria and welcomed us as a married couple. We walked through bamboo forests and hung out for hours on various beaches. We drove around, went on a helicopter ride (an incredibly generous gift from Sally's parents), ate lots of seafood, and stood in awe of the rainbows, tropical flowers, and jewel-toned mountains.

When we got back to Santa Barbara, it all felt so bittersweet. We said our goodbye to our first home together and our good friends. Within days, we packed up all our stuff and moved across the country once again, this time to Tampa, Florida.

Chapter 10

The Magic Is the Mess

Josh had found us a small one-story house for rent a few months prior to our move on a pretty brick street close to the bay. There you could watch the sun rise (getting up on time was another story). You could see swimming dolphins and stingrays alongside walkers, runners, and people on bikes and Rollerblades—it was no longer the '90s, but the hard-core Rollerbladers kept at it.

He had been wanting to move back to Florida for the last couple of years that we lived in Santa Barbara. He had grown up in Dunedin, Florida, a small town on the water, where his parents still lived, and his brother was close by. His father had a successful construction company, and Josh was ready to root down and build a career there. I knew intellectually how fortunate we were for Josh to have had such a solid opportunity that provided stability, job security, and the promise of growth and expansion, but I also wasn't exactly thrilled to be moving.

But Santa Barbara was a small town, and at times it felt too small. The idea of something new and somewhere different was also intriguing to me. I had always wanted to have children and was feeling like that time was coming and Santa Barbara was a really expensive place to make that dream come true. It helped that Kristi had moved to Tampa from San Francisco the year before, after marrying one of Josh's closest childhood friends, the one she'd been dating when she told me about Josh. I knew she would tell me where to eat, get my hair cut, and what doctors and dentists to go to. Without her there, it would have been a much harder sell for Josh. I finally grew sick of talking about an impending move and overthinking everything and became more eager and open to try it out. And after our wedding, a last hurrah of sorts, it seemed like as good a time as any.

But the move was hard. Not "hard" hard, not like losing a best friend or receiving a scary diagnosis hard, but it was challenging, and it certainly tested my patience and sanity.

There's a reason why moving is one of life's biggest stressors, I had to constantly remind myself. *A cross-country move is a huge-ass transition, and I had done it before.*

With every move, Santa Barbara being the exception, I felt like I didn't belong and didn't fit in, that I was in the wrong place, and that no one got me and my weird ways. This wasn't necessarily true, but to my detriment, it was the story I told myself.

In Tampa, I felt lost, stuck, anxious, and depressed in the beginning. Josh was back home now, living close to his family and old friends. It was his job, his family, and his religion. While he was incredibly understanding and supportive, and being home after ten years certainly had its own unique challenges, it was also familiar, and he was distracted and busy with work. I, on the other hand, felt aimless, bored, alone, and lonely as I looked for a job and friends. I couldn't find myself there. And I didn't know where to begin looking.

I missed California, and I missed us in California—the easygoing, surfing, beachy, cooking-tofu-and-going-to-yoga us. Part of me felt like I had gone backwards but also like I had aged ten years overnight. I had moved to Arizona and New Jersey for my dad's job. I didn't have a choice in the matter. And now as an adult, I had made another big move, but this time for my husband's job. *Had I made a mistake by not having a more significant career, one that would pay the bills, one that could justify me making the big decisions about where to live?*

The first folks I met in Tampa were friendly, but they seemed grown up in a way that surprised me. People were buying houses and discussing having kids, and I was desperately clinging to my freewheeling twenties for a bit longer. All of a sudden, there were work events and family obligations. Sometimes I wanted my freedom back. I missed the old me. And I missed the beach, hiking, the mountains, my friends and mentors, as well as the lack of bugs and humidity. I missed the open-mindedness and progressive nature of the West Coast. When I told people where we had moved from, they would sometimes respond with, "Why?" or "I'm so sorry." That didn't help much, but at least they understood that it felt like a colossal move.

I looked to the outside world to make it right, to make me feel better, and unfortunately, it didn't work. I still didn't understand then that looking outside myself wasn't a great strategy for finding myself. There was no place, I eventually realized, that would provide me with what I longed for. No restaurant, beach, coffee spot, bookstore, friend's house, couch, yoga studio, healer, or workplace that would make me feel at home, make me feel like I belonged. And although I was with the love of my life, my husband wasn't the answer either.

I felt a sense of shame then, too, which complicated matters, because I knew how lucky I was to have a great home, food on the table, and a husband I adored who had a reliable and well-paying job. I told myself to be grateful and to get over it, find a job, make friends, and make it work. I knew it could be worse. But also, berating oneself? Not a helpful strategy for feeling better either.

I had to stop looking for the therapist, the ultimate friend or healer, or the perfect conversation to provide me with the acceptance and connection that I yearned for. I had to stop searching outside myself and start looking within. I had a therapist whom I worked with for years in Santa Barbara.

What the hell was all this mess now? I thought I had it figured out. I had to ask myself, what was missing? What did I value, love, dream about? What still needed my attention, awareness, healing? I had to realize that I would never have it all figured out. I would be healing and learning for the rest of my life.

I had to come home to myself and cultivate my own happiness, damn it. The gurus, the Buddhist scholars, the books I read, the therapists, and above all, Glinda the Good Witch were all right: the answer was within. It's always an inside job. No one, no place, no thing could provide me with the love I wanted. The way through was to accept and learn to love myself exactly as I was.

I needed to try, as hard as it was, to stop thinking that what I needed was to change to be better. I needed to love my limitations, flaws, sensitivities, intuition, and imperfections before I could truly feel at home. I had to stop hiding, numbing, and ignoring and start feeling it all—allowing, accepting, and honoring who I was at my core, not who I thought I should be. It was like my wedding—messy, imperfect, and full of hope and love.

Chapter 11

Babies

I started volunteering at hospice in the children's grief center and was quickly offered a job as a volunteer coordinator. I interviewed and trained patient family volunteers and talked to families about how volunteers could provide respite care for the patients and caregivers when they needed a break. The volunteers I worked with were a stunning example of how good, kind, and generous human beings could be. I worked with one male volunteer who helped a brilliant eighteen-year-old woman with terminal cancer make a video for her family to watch after she died. I also worked with vigil volunteers who would sit and provide comfort and companionship to patients who were actively dying. Working at hospice put everything in perspective. I was thankful every minute of every day for my health and the health of my loved ones.

And then a year after moving to Tampa, I was pregnant. I was over the moon with excitement. I decided to wait and share the news with Rich, Kerry, and Mom, who would all be in Wales for Sally's upcoming wedding. I had told Heather over the phone and called her when, a couple of days before we were scheduled to leave for the wedding, I started spotting.

I went to the doctor, and after an ultrasound, my doctor told me he wasn't sure the pregnancy was viable. He asked me what color the bridesmaid dresses were in case I started bleeding. Fortunately, they were a dark forest green. I was about eight weeks pregnant, and the heartbeat was faint. I got home from the appointment, took it easy, but ended up miscarrying that night. It felt like terrible menstrual cramps with a lot of blood.

My husband picked up painkillers at the pharmacy, which I took, and then I cried myself to sleep. I was disappointed, scared, and so sad. Two days later, we were bound for the United Kingdom.

A miscarriage is a strange—albeit common—and particularly awful kind of loss. It's not talked about that freely or openly, but that is fortunately changing a bit. People say things in response that aren't at all comforting—things like maybe something was terribly wrong and that it was for the best. I thought about one of my favorite teachers from college who is still a friend. He would gently tell me to have compassion for people who didn't know, didn't understand, or couldn't relate. He reminded me that they weren't trying or intending to be awful, which was true; but still, miscarrying didn't feel like it was for the best. Hormones are all out of whack, and sadness seeps in, but one rarely receives flowers, cards, and food. It's lonely and awkward.

Soon enough I was pregnant again, and while I was excited, I was also terrified. Our son—our healthy, big, beautiful baby boy—Will, named after my dad, was born via an emergency C-section. I had labored at home for hours, and when I couldn't handle the pain anymore, even though my contractions were erratic, Josh took me to the hospital.

I opted for an epidural, needing a break from the intensity of the twisting, gripping contractions; but soon after the injection, I was so relaxed I fell asleep. I woke up after a brief nap and hours of more contractions—these I couldn't really feel. After a few attempts at pushing, my heart rate and Will's heartbeat were all over the map. My doctor was concerned, sensing that our baby boy was experiencing distress, and suggested a C-section. Within minutes of having the conversation, I was being prepped for surgery. It was surreal and frightening.

The room was sterile and bright, with lots of additional nurses and doctors in scrubs and masks. All of a sudden, time was moving rapidly. As I lay waiting for surgery, I was scared but also beyond thankful that I would get to meet my son so soon. I was in love and in awe when I heard him cry for the first time, and as soon as I held him, my heart leaped out of my chest, eyes, and nose. The labor and delivery had been difficult, and I was exhausted. My body was shaking violently and buzzing from the drugs and adrenaline coursing through my system. I was crying, and Josh was crying.

Within minutes Josh went with Will to the nursery while the doctors and nurses finished stitching me up. Soon enough I was in recovery, and after an hour, I was in my room trying to nurse. I had no idea what I was doing, and it was so much more difficult than I thought it would be. I had taken a breastfeeding class and hoped it would be second nature, but it wasn't, at least not for me. Nurses and lactation consultants tried to help, literally grabbing my sore boobs and showing me how to hold them while cradling my baby's soft head. But my nipples hurt like Hades until I got the hang of it. Changing diapers was eye-opening too. I'd get peed on, and sometimes I thought my son had a leak because when I picked him up, he was often wet. Turns out it's important to have things pointing in the right direction.

After getting home, I didn't know whether to read the reference books regarding eating, sleeping, and schedules or simply to wing it. Everyone had advice as to how to do things, and it was overwhelming. I didn't find my groove until I stopped trying so hard and trusted my intuition over everyone else's opinions.

I loved it when Will slept in my arms and on my chest. I also loved when Josh would come home from work and hold him so I could move around more freely again. I adored playing with baby Will and taking him to the park, and I also loved having help from my mom when she visited and from my mother-in-law, Nancy, who would come by, do laundry, and take care of him so I could nap, take a walk, or go grocery shopping unencumbered.

The responsibility of keeping this sweet little being alive, whom I loved and cared for in such a deep, primal way, rocked my world. It was difficult, and I could do it. It was exhausting and exhilarating, and while I perpetually needed a break, a glass of water, or a nap, I also never wanted to be without him. Parenting was full-on and full of contradictions.

When Will was eight months old, I earned a certification to teach yoga. I chose not to go back to work at hospice, and while I was grateful to have had a choice in the matter and thrilled to be able to be home with him, I also felt isolated and lonely once again. I longed for meaning and connection outside my house, outside mothering and partnering. I knew this was an incredibly important job I was doing, but I wondered if there was a job I could do outside my house too. Josh and I found a therapist who helped us ease into the transition of parenthood. Outside help from an empathetic mental health professional and teaching yoga, even if it was just a couple times a week, provided me with a bit more space to breathe, be, stretch, feel, use my brain, and move while in community and connection with other adults.

Between giving birth to my son and then my daughter three years later, I had another miscarriage. It was, of course, upsetting the second time around, but because of a scheduled D&C, the procedure used to dilate the cervix and remove fetal tissue, the experience was a lot less physically painful and also less emotionally taxing. I felt taken care of by a physician who performed the procedure with care and compassion. I was sad but also knew that this go-around, I could carry a pregnancy to term. I had friends going through IVF, friends who got pregnant easily, and friends who adopted. No matter what their particular situation was, starting a family was an emotional roller coaster. Looking back now, I realize just how intense it all was.

My daughter, Phoebe, came flying into the world twenty-five minutes after I arrived at the hospital. It couldn't have been a more different labor from the one I had with Will. I was hoping to have a vaginal birth this time around. I had done my research and talked to different doctors, midwives, and doulas and eventually switched practices and hospitals, choosing to go to a teaching hospital in the area that was more aligned with my values and dreams of having a VBAC (vaginal birth after cesarean). I wanted to avoid having surgery, if at all possible, but was certainly on board if that was what was needed for my and my baby's health.

I labored at home while walking, sitting, and breathing on an exercise ball while watching one of my favorite shows, *Sex and the City*. While I viewed Samantha having liberating sex, my mind was delightfully distracted and I could relax. I had one momentous contraction where she must have changed positions while I was in the bath. After that I turned into a wild animal. I felt the strongest urge to push right there in the bathroom and then again on the family room floor, much to Josh's surprise and horror. He was a nervous wreck and understandably did not want me to have the baby at home.

It all happened so fast. My friend Rebecca down the street came to watch Will, who was asleep in a sleeping bag on the floor next to our bedroom. We didn't want him to sleep in our room, so this was the compromise we made with our three-year-old son. I couldn't find shoes, so I arrived at the hospital shoeless. I was put in a wheelchair by an aide and tried to breathe through jolts of electric pain, knowing that if I froze or got scared, my body would resist the process, making surgery all the more likely.

A little boy near the elevators looked at me and said to his mom enthusiastically, "Look, Mom, that lady is about to have a baby."

I was on a hospital bed with no time left for drugs, and before I knew it, my beautiful little baby girl was wrapped up in the white, pink, and blue blankets in my arms and suckling merrily.

I was on cloud nine and so in love with her little features and the slightest tinge of red in her hair.

While celebrating the arrival of Phoebe, I was simultaneously worrying about my mom. The summer before Phoebe was born, while visiting New Jersey, my mom was diagnosed at age sixty-nine with breast cancer. We had gone to the beach one morning, and while Will played happily in the sand, I sat in a chair in the sun, resting my hands on my large belly and chatting with Rich and Kerry. We were waiting for my mom to come back to the beach from an appointment when she called to tell us that during her routine mammogram, the radiologist saw something he didn't like. He felt certain that it was cancer. In the upcoming months, she had a lumpectomy, chemo, and radiation, handling it all with a smile on her face and as if it was nothing more than a small bump in the road.

Chapter 12

Secrets

It was the first night of a ten-day seminar for my graduate study in transpersonal psychology—a field of psychology combining the study of humanistic psychology, human development, wisdom traditions, consciousness, and spirituality. I was thirty-six at the time, and Will and Phoebe were six and three. I had felt like a seeker for a long time. I was interested in the mysterious, meaningful, and unifying aspect of humanity. I had thought many times about becoming a mental health therapist and started a graduate program in counseling psychology when I first moved to Tampa. But I dropped out after the first quarter, having found it difficult to keep up with coursework while working a full-time job at hospice. I had studied Reiki, massage therapy, and taught yoga. I had read books on Zen Buddhism and read my fair share of self-help books. But I yearned for something else too. I yearned to help others while helping myself. I set out to become a life coach and study the importance of creative expression, stress management, and spiritual growth and healing.

The initial in-person seminar for my program at Sofia University took place in the majestic redwoods in Palo Alto, California. Phoebe and Will stayed with my mom in New Jersey while Kerry and Richard were on hand to help out, especially during bath and mealtime. Josh was home working and taking care of the house and our dog, Poppy. I missed them all, but I was beyond excited for a solo adventure and to be participating in a program that spoke so directly to my soul.

At one point in the evening, during a group exercise, I sat with a woman who had wisdom and kindness spilling from her eyes. Susan was long, lean, lanky, and older than me by about twenty years. Her silver slivers of hair reminded me of the moon. She was delicate like a bird, as if she belonged outside singing, flitting from branch to branch, and not inside under fluorescent lights.

She had a woundedness that I felt drawn to, a realness. If you have ever heard of the term *wounded healer*, she embodied it. She was living with a serious chronic illness, and maybe because of it, she was incredibly perceptive, intuitive, compassionate, and kind. She had dedicated her life to healing—herself as well as others.

I felt a familiar sadness surface while talking to her. A sadness I had tried to hear, heal, and sometimes even squelch. This sweet, wise angel bird Susan noticed. I told her that it felt old, embedded. Maybe it had been there since I was a child and took hold when my dad died. It felt like grief but not the grief of losing my dad. I had done a lot of therapy in my twenties around his death, and while I missed him every single day and the hurt never completely goes away, it didn't pierce me to talk about it anymore.

I told Susan about the abortion. The experience still stung. Like there was residual shame and stickiness attached to it. It wasn't just the fact that it happened and that it was an awful thing to have gone through at seventeen so close to my dad's death but that it was still a secret. When I told Susan that I had kept this secret from my mom for eighteen years, she encouraged me to tell her. She said that by not having the conversation, I was missing an opportunity for an authentic connection. I was cutting my mom off from her own growth too. I knew she was right. I knew secrets were poison and that it was time to get it off my chest and release any shame around it once and for all.

When my mom came to Tampa the next winter, we headed to the beach for a few days. I asked her if she wanted to join me for a walk on the beach. It was midday on a Saturday in February— quiet and cool, sunny and breezy.

Josh was sitting on a towel, hands in the sand, water close to his feet as he dug holes with the kids and built sandcastles.

I had been planning on having this conversation for such a long time that I had rehearsed what I was going to say and how I would say it. I didn't want her to feel bad or guilty. I only hoped it would open a door for connection and understanding.

I didn't want to carry this secret anymore. I was ready to drop it, to leave it all out there on the earth and let the magic of the soil eat it up and transform it into something with wings.

I was done with shame.

I had told my siblings and many of my close friends about what had happened over the years. And no one had left me because of it. That was my fear—that if I told the truth, I'd be unlovable, bad, wrong. But when I voiced out loud what I was ashamed of, no one was mad at me. No one close to me stopped loving me because of it. Maybe they even loved me more because they knew me better.

I was nervous, tongue-tied, and a bit flushed, although I convinced myself that maybe it was the sun resting on my cheeks. I could feel the air between us and the weight of heavy things unsaid.

As we walked near the soft lapping of the waves, on the powdery sand, her white chinos rolled up and with red nails and her charm bracelet jangling as we walked along, I said to her, "I have something I've wanted to tell you for a long time.

Don't worry, everything is okay now. I don't know why it feels so important for me to get this off my chest now, but it feels like the right timing. I don't like secrets, and I don't want to keep this from you any longer. When I was seventeen, I got pregnant and had an abortion. I didn't tell anyone other than Erica and eventually my boyfriend when he got home from a trip out West. He took me to Planned Parenthood to get it done. You had so much going on with Dad's death and me still in high school and living in a new town that I didn't want to put any more on your plate. I was too worried something bad would happen to you too."

Exhale.

She said, "I understand. I'm sorry you had to go through that. I'm sorry I wasn't there, but I understand that these things happen. I was a teenager too."

We walked in awkward silence for a brief spell. There wasn't much else to say. I felt relief, and also . . . I craved more. More what? Questions. Tears. Connection.

Then she said, "I'm going to head back to the room to use the bathroom."

"Oh okay. Are you okay? Is it because of what I told you?"

"No, not at all. I completely understand. Really, I'm not mad or upset. I love you."

That was that.

What was I expecting?

She wasn't mad at me. Or upset. She really wasn't. She said she understood. Wasn't that enough?

The next day driving in the car . . .

"Mom, I hope your stomach wasn't upset by what I told you."

"No, not at all, I really do understand, and I'm sorry. I know that must have been hard. "

What did I want to hear?

I'm sorry you were alone. That must have been terrifying! And on the heels of losing your dad in such an awful way. You were brave, and I'm proud of you. I'M SO PROUD of you.

Was it painful? How was it when it happened? Was he there for you? Do you think about it still? Do you have regrets? It was the right decision. It's hard being a woman bearing all these burdens. And alone. That must have been one of the hardest decisions you've ever had to make. How did you feel then? How do you feel now? I know you must have been sad because I know you've always wanted to be a mom. Nothing is easy. Life is hard no matter what.

I love you. I love you. I love you. Thank you for telling me.

All at once, I was a teenager going shopping with her at the mall holding a Clearly Canadian in my hands. I was her little girl asking for another kiss, two more kisses, before bed. I'd say, "Who do you love?" in a silly voice, and she'd respond in the same silly voice, "Everybody." I was her big girl staying out late and coming home after drinking. I was her adventure-seeker traveling the world, her pretty bride, the mother of her grandkids. I was her adult daughter sensing that we didn't have all that much time left together.

She loved me so much. I knew it. I had always known it. And yet I wanted to hear her say it. More. Why? Because it felt good.

This would be enough. It had to be.

I felt lighter. But also perplexed. Why didn't I feel relieved completely?

Sometimes we seek resolution and hope to get it during conversations with other people. But I think the conversations that are most cathartic and life-changing are the ones we have with ourselves. And it's good to know that we can always go back and say the things that we needed to hear to ourselves. We love ourselves that way.

I promised to love the heck out of my kids, to tell them I love them, to hug and kiss them even when they're teenagers, to be open, to talk to them about the stakes of having sex too soon. To tell them how I'm feeling. To ask how they're feeling.

I promised to love myself and the lost, scared, grieving seventeen-year-old girl who for a split second thought maybe it would be better if it all ended.

But I didn't give up then. And I won't now. There's too much to love. And too much love to give. My mom loved me. I loved her. And I love me.

All of me.

Faults, flaws, mistakes, and all, I love her.

I turn inward and hug my glowing, beating heart. I love the little soul we gave up and the ones that followed from two miscarriages.

This secret was eating away at my insides, and now it wasn't.

And as uncomfortable as transparency can be, it feels cleaner, healthier to have it all out on the table. I don't want to hide. There's something about mothering ourselves—speaking up for ourselves, what we believe in, what our hearts yearn for, what we need—and this was that for me. It had very little to do with my mom and what she said. It was about my heart and my voice. I felt freer. There cannot be peace without freedom. And I hoped there was peace there for her too.

Chapter 13

Circles

I started leading circles when my friend Shaun, from grad school, asked me what I wanted to be when I grew up. I had just graduated with my master's degree in transpersonal psychology and was figuring out what I was going to do with all that I had learned and experienced in the two-year program. What Shaun actually asked me on the phone that day was, "If you could do anything for work, what would that look like?"

I didn't think. I closed my eyes and felt what I felt. I told him that I wanted to create a warm and welcoming space for women to come sit and be vulnerable, brave, and open with the hopes of finding more connection, creativity, fulfillment, meaning, and healing. We'd be supportive and encouraging. We'd talk about what mattered most. If we needed to cry, we'd cry without apology. If laughter was what was called for, we'd laugh without restraint. We'd listen to one another without judgment and without offering advice. We'd learn from each other's experiences and practice honesty, courage, mindfulness, empathy, and taking long, deep breaths together. We'd erase shame and free ourselves from guilt. Maybe we'd make art, sing, dance, journal, and do some yoga together too. Collaboration over comparison. It didn't matter as long as we showed up authentically and shared from our hearts.

I taught yoga for years and found that what I really wanted to do was not tell people to strike a pose but ask them how they were feeling in their bodies. Along with writing my blog, I had a strong desire to help people not so much as a teacher but more as a cocreator. I knew how helpful being in a group with a set intention could be from a women's spirituality group

I had participated in when Will was a baby. I found it hugely comforting and nurturing during the difficult transition to motherhood.

Shaun responded on the phone that day with, "I think you should do it. What do you have to lose?"

I knew he was right. I knew the details didn't have to all be ironed out. I needed to just put it out there and show up and see who showed up for the invitation. I contacted the yoga studio I used to teach at, and the owner of the studio, my friend Annie, let me use the space and signed herself up to attend my very first Sacred Soul Women's Circle. The first circle met once a month in the evening for ninety minutes. Within a matter of days of posting an invitation on social media but mostly through word of mouth, seven women had signed up. It was a practice in being the change I wished to see in the world. If I yearned for this kind of connection, I knew I couldn't be the only one.

Twelve years later, I'm still facilitating my Sacred Soul circles. Many of the same women come back repeatedly, but in every circle, there are at least one to two new participants. I welcome women, of all ages and backgrounds, and I tell them the only obligation is to come with an open heart and to make every attempt to come to every session in the name of consistency and support to the other women in the group.

In one session this past fall, my friend brought her three-year-old daughter, and another friend was there with her mother. I sat with tears in my eyes, seeing how things have grown and changed over the years and loving that there was a sixty-year age difference between the youngest and the oldest participants. I love it when women of all different ages are there together.

We've ebbed and flowed and made changes when needed. During the pandemic, we tried Zoom circles. They weren't ideal, but they were something! We cooked, painted, meditated, and journaled together. We shared our fears and our dreams.

As scientific studies show repeatedly, social isolation is bad for our health. Even worse than smoking cigarettes. When we come together, the hard shit in life feels more manageable. Hearing "Me too" and "I get it" and "We're rooting for you" is seriously soothing to our frayed nerves . . . and our broken and fearful hearts.

I'm forever grateful to the women who have come to the circles and the art, writing, and yoga retreats I've led with my two partners, Katie and Charlotte, at our annual Joyful Reset. Their openness and willingness to hold this kind of sacred space together is inspiring to witness and be a part of. It gives me faith that anything is possible. Circles and groups are as old as humanity, and whether we're sitting around a fire, sharing a meal together, or being in a group as a way to cope with loss or addiction, sharing our truths and stories with each other is deeply healing and transformative.

Recently, a woman in a circle said, "So much has become clearer in the past six weeks, it's wild, and it's not like this is rocket science."

I laughed because it's not complicated, but it is big.

We yearn to be seen, heard, validated. We want our stories to matter. We seek something deep, real, universal, and sacred. We can let down our guards. We can make meaning. We're much more than our limitations and losses, and we're already whole. There is no such thing as perfection, whether we're discussing a relationship or an individual.

A friend and teacher once told me that when women come together in intentional spaces such as these, spaces full of compassion, we release feel-good hormones like oxytocin. There is a real sense of lift and hope that swirls around us at the end of a gathering, keeping us bound together with a sense of promise and friendship.

Writing down and sharing our stories is a big part of the magic that transpires in these circles. We're social creatures wired for connection, and we thrive from bonds that help us navigate the full spectrum of emotions and experiences. We're reminded of our similarities (as opposed to our differences) and our ability to adjust, accept, and keep going when circumstances challenge us. We remember how much there is to celebrate. We need each other in a myriad of ways, and everything is infinitely better when we come together in the spirit of collaboration.

We complicate things so much as humans, but circles are simple. We show up. We wake up. We listen. We share. We laugh and cry. We write, play, and feel. We breathe. We learn and grow. We keep going.

Part II

We are not broken by our trauma;
we are broken open.

– Parker Palmer

Chapter 14

Anticipatory Grief

Will was eight and Phoebe five when we celebrated my mom's seventy-fifth birthday on a Caribbean Island along with Heather and her husband, Jim, and my niece, Maggie (the youngest of four and only girl in the family). Rich, and his partner, Marshall, and Kerry and her wife at the time were there too, and they had flown in from New Jersey with my mom. It was the first night of our vacation, and normally, I would have enjoyed a banana daiquiri, a piña colada, or a margarita by then. But standing on the beach at the bar right after sunset with my mom, I ordered water.

"Really?" she asked, her voice climbing an octave higher. *Happy birthday, Mom!*

She had been telling anyone who would listen about how we should have a third child.

"I think three is a nice number," she would say to her mailman, dentist, book group, bridge club, old friends, dry cleaner, and of course, Josh and me. And when our neighbor friends had their third baby, she was ecstatic and hoped it was contagious.

For years Josh and I debated. I was scared, having had two previous miscarriages and knowing that my "advanced maternal age" would put me in the high-risk category. But there was a strong internal pull that I couldn't ignore.

Our third dreamy little nugget was born two weeks early, the day after Will turned nine. Her big sister, Phoebe, was six, the same age difference between me and my big sister Kerry.

One night while I was nursing Izzy in her lavender-and-gray bedroom, listening to a CD of Spanish guitar, sleep hung in the air like a low mist. Josh was reading books to Will and Phoebe in the room next door as my eyes got increasingly heavy. Although that warm little squish was heaven in my arms, I couldn't wait to crawl into my own bed and get underneath my covers where I'd stick one foot out (both in felt claustrophobic; both out felt too exposed).

My phone rang, and when I saw it was from my mom, my heart dropped into my stomach. She was at her friend Jill's house in New Jersey, about forty-five minutes from where she lived on the shore. Jill and my mom had been friends since they were nine years old and grew up in Maplewood, a storybook neighborhood with a pond that froze in the winter. They had the same sense of humor, and Jill would often preface a story with, "I'm going straight to hell." I adore Jill—also known as Aunt Jill, or "my mom's little friend, Jill."

My mom never called at 9:00 p.m. But that night was different as we were waiting for results from a recent scan. She had had some discomfort in her neck that she noticed soon after Izzy was born. That night on the phone, she told me that the cancer had spread to her bone and liver. It was six years after her initial breast cancer diagnosis. It all felt eerily familiar. The summer before Phoebe was born, my mom began treatment for breast cancer. A year later, during a colonoscopy, they found cancer again. She had surgery and had been given a clean bill of health for the past three years.

But a year after my mom's breast cancer had returned, I found myself sitting by the window in the hospital in Red Bank, New Jersey, staring at the river shrouded in low clouds as my mom lay sleeping. The cancer had then spread to her brain, and after completing the most recent round of radiation, she was unsteady on her feet. She had fallen at home trying to get to the doorbell, which was what had landed her in the hospital. Hours turned into days without answers or guidance. Kerry, Rich, and I took turns going to the hospital, doing errands, and taking care of my mom's black cocker spaniel, Betty, as well as her house. While Josh was home with the kids, I was with my mom, missing them and also grateful to be with her.

That morning, as I sat by her bed feeling unsure and scared, an unfriendly female doctor came in. Without so much as a greeting, she asked me flatly if I would like her to make a referral to hospice. It was such an intense question to spring on me so nonchalantly, as if she were asking me if I liked licorice. My mom still wanted to try chemo. For the third time. That was the one option left. But there is no cure for metastatic breast cancer, so there wasn't a lot of hope.

I believed in the mission of hospice care. While working and volunteering there, I loved the idea of helping the whole family and not just the patient. It was about honoring the wishes of the patient by keeping them comfortable, pain-free, and ideally, at home. I had wondered silently if it was time for her to stop treatment and go on hospice because it felt like it was one medical nightmare after the next, and we seemed to be arriving at one closed door after another.

But did she really only have six months left to live? Was there nothing else they could do for her? It all felt so abrupt. No one had told us anything. It was like we were waiting but we weren't sure what we were waiting for. My siblings and I were kept in the dark, and we kept missing her doctors when they did their rounds at the hospital. It was so frustrating. I would be there all day, leave for an hour to get a sandwich, only to come back and find out that once again, the doctor had just been in and was now long gone.

Finally, an oncologist called us one night while Kerry, Richard, Marshall, and I were hanging out at Rich and Marshall's house. It was the night after hospice had been suggested. We had just eaten pizza, had a few drinks in us, and were draped over the couch, exhausted, and not in the mood to have a conversation with a doctor we had never met.

The phone rang, and we all looked at one another pleadingly.

"Fine." I finally stood up and quickly rehearsed silently what I was going to say.

I often feel nervous when I talk to doctors. My heart beats faster, and my face flushes. I don't want to piss anyone off or ask the wrong questions. The leftover people pleaser in me wants them to like me and think I'm a good girl. This was not her oncologist on the phone, the one she liked so much, but another from the same practice. The last name of this doctor? Laughinghouse. That's right. An oncologist with the last name Laughinghouse.

"You gotta be kidding me," I muttered to myself.

Dr. Laughinghouse told me he didn't agree with the hospital doctor who had referred my mom to hospice.

"We don't want to give up on her yet," he said. "We need time to see if the radiation is working." Though it certainly didn't seem like it was.

But isn't this cancer incurable? I thought to myself. How much longer would we torture her with treatment that wouldn't save her? There was no conversation about preserving quality of life or what her wishes were, and I wondered, if my mom could think clearly, would she really want to live like this?

I didn't want to give up on my mom either. His word choice pissed me off. I felt like a cold, heartless jerk for even asking him about hospice. But part of me also knew it was probably the kindest, most helpful thing to do at this stage. That was when I'd leave my heart and intuition to the side and think maybe this wasn't the end after all. Maybe she would make it down to Florida again. To my son's bar mitzvah. To see our baby girl turn two. We would all smile and be relieved and so thankful for how my mom continued to survive against all odds. "She's such a fighter, a survivor," people would say. We'd raise our glasses and toast her when we gathered at the beach to celebrate another birthday.

This is how it was. One minute, what we dreaded was actually happening right in front of our face, but then the next minute, hope flooded the room, and I felt ashamed of thinking about her death.

At that point, she was still saying she was looking forward to traveling in the fall to Palm Springs with her bridge friends. She wanted to get up to Nantucket to see Heather and Maggie in the summer. She wanted to buy new clothes and a pair of shoes similar to the ones Heather had on recently. *Confusion caused by the progression of her disease? Denial? Hope?* We didn't know.

Before the cancer spread to her brain (spots, she would call them), before three weeks of "whole-brain radiation," before the fall, before she tried yet another final round of chemo that had made her feel miserable, my siblings and I would talk on the phone trying to figure out what to do. We were doing the best we could, but we felt lost. We missed our dad. We were adults but felt like children.

I went back and forth from Tampa to my mom's house in New Jersey a lot those days, and it was exhausting. I also knew how lucky I was that I had the resources to fly so often and the support at home from my husband, Nancy, babysitters, and friends. When I was in New Jersey, I'd try to cook a few meals even though I'm terrible at cooking and don't really enjoy it. I tried to bring love and not fear and anxiety into the room with me. I'd give Rich and Kerry a break since they lived in New Jersey near my mom and were doing all the caretaking when I wasn't around. Heather and I were doing what we could from a distance and visiting often, but it was nothing compared to the daily check-ins and constant worry that Kerry and Richard, who lived locally, dealt with.

I was bombarded with how to preserve her and our memories together with thoughts like, *I should record her voice. I have one message from her on my voicemail on my phone. I wish I had more.* Now when I scroll through my voice messages, I wonder if I should keep random ones from friends and family just in case that person gets sick or dies suddenly.

Every time I went home to visit her, she was less there. Diminished in so many different ways. After that week in the hospital, she was moved to a rehab facility for two weeks to try and get stronger for further treatment. The tightness in my chest hurt. I had felt it before. It was heartbreak. I was missing her, grieving her, even though she was still there.

Chapter 15

Toasted Brioche with Avocado

It felt like everything was careening toward the end, and I wanted to be with my mom as much as possible. I needed a lot of help at home and relied heavily on my family to be able to make the frequent trips to New Jersey. My mother-in-law, Nancy was an absolute rock star and helped with everything and anything, including heaps of laundry, school pickups, meals, errands, and watching Izzy. I couldn't have done it without my friends too, who dropped off food and checked in on me via texts and phone calls.

Filling up on the thankfulness was an antidote to the heartache and crushing stress I was feeling. I'd wake up overwhelmed and exhausted, open my front door, and find a Borgia—a latte with honey, citrus, and homemade whipped cream from my favorite coffee shop, Jet City Espresso—on my doorstep. An invitation to go out for lunch or a walk meant so much to me even if I rarely was able to accept the offer.

Those kindnesses were like fresh oxygen breathing peace and glimmers of okayness into my days. I felt held, supported, and ushered by some mysterious force. I felt connected, and although I sometimes felt lonely, I knew I wasn't alone. When friends asked how they could help, I'd always think of something.

I also engaged in lots of little rituals like lighting candles; listening to peaceful music; buying myself bright-colored flowers; and closing my eyes, pausing, and taking slow, deep breaths. Basking in nothingness and everythingness as I held Izzy tightly in my arms gave me life. I'd smell her sweet head and drink in her smile before putting her down for a nap. I'd look out the window and savor whatever beautiful sight I noticed in my backyard. Often it was a cardinal, its red feathers vibrant against the green leaves and blue sky. I moved slowly and deliberately. All these things helped anchor me to the present moment unfolding before my eyes.

In the span of a month, my siblings and I went from having a conversation about hiring someone to help with cooking and meal prep to needing a full-time caregiver and, soon enough, hospice. Verna was the caregiver we hired after my mom came home from the rehab facility, where her roommate constantly sang in Italian. My mom never wanted a caregiver living with her, and we obliged until there was no other option.

But before my mom could come home, she needed a place to be on the first floor of the house. Heather and my Uncle Doug, my dad's youngest brother, turned the bonus room—with its wood-paneled walls, hot tub, and big windows—into a peaceful white room with a hospital bed. We knew how fortunate we were to be able to do all this and that so many people would have the only option of putting their loved ones in a facility or having to quit their jobs to be the caregivers.

It was strange at first, spending all our time in this room where we rarely hung out before, but the transformation was stunning and made everything easier. My mom could look out at the backyard blooming with dogwoods and see deer nibbling on her pale blue and purple hydrangeas in the summer. Hanging on one of the tree branches was a hummingbird feeder with sugar water that Marshall filled regularly.

I remember once while watching *Kathie Lee & Hoda* on TV, my mom said, "I never watched this at home."

I didn't correct her. While she was home, I realized it didn't always feel that way.

Verna, the caregiver we hired, made sure my mom was eating and drinking. She'd also rub cocoa butter on her bare scalp ("soft like a baby's bottom," my brother would say), feet, arms, legs, and hands. She knew to not use too much or rub too hard and disrupt her skin, which was as fragile as tissue paper. She'd get my mom undressed and dressed so gingerly to avoid any possibility of hurting her. She gave her sponge baths, brushed her teeth, and administered her medicine mixed with applesauce.

In the afternoon, Verna brought her snacks like "pretzel crisps"—the flat, crunchy pretzels—in the blue-and-white bag that she'd put in a bowl. Maybe we'd watch a movie together like *La La Land* or, if the kids were with me, *Beauty and the Beast*.

I thought a lot about my friend Phyllis then. I met her when I volunteered for hospice in college in Santa Barbara. I gave her hand massages and Reiki, an energetic healing modality known for helping people deeply relax. Phyllis, in her midsixties with silver hair, blue eyes, and a knowing smile, taught me about Tonglen—a Buddhist practice of acknowledging the pain you are feeling while using it as a prayer to ease the suffering of others. It was so completely selfless and mind-blowing to me that during her tremendous pain, she was still so concerned about helping others. It brought meaning and purpose to her suffering. I was in my early twenties then and a bit of a "Nervous Nellie" (an expression my mom often used). Phyllis was always more concerned about my comfort than her own. I felt blessed beyond belief to be with her. I felt like I was spending precious time with an angel, a wise prophet, and a deeply spiritual soul with an abundance of wisdom to share from a life well lived.

She once told me a story about going to Lourdes, France, a pilgrimage site known for its healing waters. Phyllis went there after her first cancer diagnosis. She told me about the helpers, the women who assisted her out of the private bath and got her dressed. They did so with such care and concern it brought tears to her eyes and mine as she retold the story. The intimacy of this gesture, the slowing down, the softness, the tender attention to every detail made her feel cared for and unconditionally valued and loved. I visited Lourdes and its healing waters after I graduated from college, wanting to witness the miraculous pilgrimage site for myself. I bought a little container of the water from a tourist shop and brought some back for Phyllis.

I often thought about the writing of Henri J. M. Nouwen, whom Phyllis introduced me to when my mom was sick. Here is a passage from his book, *Our Greatest Gift: A Meditation on Dying and Caring,* that I love:

> The real question before our death, then, is not, "How much can I still accomplish," or "How much influence can I still exert?" but, "How can I live so that I can continue to be fruitful when I am no longer here among my family and friends?" That question shifts our attention from doing to being. Our doing brings success, but our being bears fruit. The great paradox of our lives is that we are often concerned about what we do or still can do, but we are most likely to be remembered for who we were. If the Spirit guides our lives—the Spirit of love, joy, peace, gentleness, forgiveness, courage, perseverance, hope, and faith—then that Spirit will not die but will continue to grow from generation to generation.

Simply put, Phyllis taught me just how beautiful and fruitful the end of life could be.

I yearned for the long-gone carefree days of sauntering down the burgundy-carpeted stairs at my mom's house in an extra-large T-shirt from college and pajama pants. I'd come down into the kitchen to see my mom sitting at the kitchen table, checking her email and telling me about a "silly" forward from one of the bridge gals. She had a little magnifying mirror with tweezers nearby, and she'd put on her reading glasses with a pursed mouth, talking to me while plucking unwanted hairs from her chin.

I'd feel excited about what the day had in store. If this feeling was a season, it would be summer: cocktails in the evening, lightning bugs, sunsets, corn on the cob, juicy red tomatoes, and the beach club with a strange sign that said, "No Bouncing Balls or We'll Bust Yours." But it was also Christmas morning: excitement, no place to go and no place I'd rather be, presents waiting under a glistening tree, the fire in the fireplace, my Aunt Barbara's eggnog, cozy on the couch with a warm blankie watching a Christmas movie like *Elf* or *The Family Stone* for the hundredth time.

She would also often tell me about her plans for the day. Maybe she was going to get her hair done or see if Andrea could fix her nails. Or she had to go to the bank, the post office, the dry cleaner. And I knew that in all the places she went, people would be so happy to see her, to bask in the warmth of her—my mom in her big, black wool coat with the furry hood over a kelly green sweater. Often it was the cardigan I gave her one Christmas from Oprah's store in Chicago. The one she wore so much she had to get the elbows patched. Her typical uniform was a green sweater in winter or her pink polo and white shorts in the summer. She'd have on her super-soft leather driving shoes, red lipstick, and silver clip-on earrings while complaining that her hair was like butter. But she always looked so put-together, a trait unfortunately not passed on to me.

Now the kitchen table was no longer used for meals, checking emails, or catching up. It served as "command central" with Ziploc bags full of medication and stacks of important papers from her hospice team.

My mom in a hospital bed waiting for Verna to change and feed her reminded me of the way Izzy waited for me to pick her up from her crib in the morning.

Verna would sing, "Good morning, Susie."

My mom would beam back at her, "Good morning." Sometimes she would even giggle a little.

So sad and so sweet, so much so that my heart felt like it might pop out of my chest or come out of my mouth.

Sometimes I'd help Verna change her Depends and clothes in the morning.

And as Verna gently turned my mom on her side, speaking encouragingly and lovingly, I'd put my lips to her impossibly soft cheek, and my mom would sometimes say she was sick and tired of what was happening or that she was bored. It was heartbreaking to witness. She was such a good sport about the whole thing, something she would have said to me when I was a little girl on the way home from a checkup at the doctor.

Sometimes I'd read on the couch next to her hospital bed and fall asleep. It was peaceful in that room. Sometimes it felt like we were avoiding something or waiting for something, and sometimes it felt just right. It was all incredibly sad but bursting with love too. And it was real and truthful, which made it beautiful. Sometimes I'd feel helpless, but then I'd remember that being present, loving, compassionate, and gentle *was* something, and it was big.

At first my mom drank her beloved instant coffee still, but when it became too hard on her stomach, she switched to Lipton black tea with a spoonful of sugar. Verna poured her tea in a dainty white cup painted with sunflowers and bees that my mom bought.

"I thought these were so pretty, I got them from that cute little place in Spring Lake," I could hear her say, although she wouldn't say it now because she was so tired and didn't say as much.

Verna would always lay a floral place mat on the wooden tray and then place the white plate with the blue rim for Mom's avocado toast with the napkin perfectly folded into a neat triangle.

Now, when I make my kids avocado toast on brioche with lime and sea salt, I think about my mom. I think about Verna and all the beautiful, time-stopping, joy-enhancing details. Paying attention was all we had. It was everything.

Chapter 16

When Pets and People Die

I met my friend Rebecca for lunch on a rainy Sunday afternoon. Rebecca had moved to Boulder a few years before, and it was balm for my soul to be sitting with her again in Tampa. She used to live right down the street, and when I all but gave birth to Phoebe in my family room, Rebecca was the one who came over to stay with Will who was sound asleep at the time so we could rush to the hospital.

That day with Rebecca, I ordered a salad but should have just eaten the double-espresso cookies from Pane Rustica, one of my favorite restaurants in Tampa. The salad I nibbled on sat in my stomach like an unattended garden, all weeds and roots.

I had been home in Tampa for only about a week before I started planning my next trip to New Jersey. I ached to be there with my mom. But when I was there without the kids and Josh, I ached to be home with them. I wasn't sure if I should go solo or bring the kids this next trip. Things were progressing quickly, and while I wanted her to see them and for them to spend as much time with her as possible, my thoughts were jumbled as I wondered if it would be too much for my mom if I brought all three kids. Would the kids feel frightened, overwhelmed, too sad? Was this how they would remember her? Not the soft-skinned, put-together grandmother with colorful shirts, red lipstick, and clip-on earrings? Though she was completely bed-bound, she still smiled radiantly and rosily when they were in the room.

The last time I was there with everybody, only about a month prior, I played a song to make her laugh. Will, Phoebe, and I had made a delicious, albeit ridiculous, discovery one afternoon. The two of them were yelling at our Alexa to play something. Will wanted to hear The Shins, and Phoebe demanded Taylor Swift. I was so sick of their yelling and Alexa lighting up and saying, "I don't know that one," that in a weak moment, I shouted at Alexa to play the "Penis Song." I didn't know there was such a thing, but lo and behold, a song came on in a barbershop quartet style that went, "When life gets you down / Keeps you wearing a frown / And the gravy train has left you behind . . ." Then "I take a look at my enormous penis / And my troubles start a-meltin' away."

At that, we fell to the ground. We were doubled over with laughter and disbelief. As Izzy used to say when she was little, it was not "'propriate." We played the song for my mom while Phoebe danced and Will shook his head trying not to laugh.

My mom said, "What is this?" And then sarcastically, she said, "Oh, this is wonderful," while giggling . . .

Back to the lunch with a teary-eyed Rebecca. She recounted the story of being told as a child that she had to stay home while her younger brother visited their dying grandfather in the hospital. As she struggled with anger over her dad's decision, her grandfather died right after her brother's visit. Her words cut deep. That could very well be the last time my kids saw my mom. Rebecca encouraged me to integrate their experience as part of a bigger picture that paints death not as separate from but part of life. Messy and honest, sad and real.

After our lunch, I went home and walked into our closet and saw the poem Josh had hung on the wall: "Make the Ordinary Come Alive" by William Martin. Immediately, my eyes were drawn to the line "Show them how to cry when pets and people die."

The kids and I arrived at my mom's a week later. I watched Phoebe stare at my mom's shaking hands, and again I wondered if this was too upsetting and confusing. But then she asked me to pick her up so she could give my mom a kiss on her cheek. Another day Will chose to stay home and keep "Susie" company while the rest of us went out to lunch. One night before bed, I lifted Izzy up to kiss my mom good night. In her powder-smelling jammies and diaper-clad bottom, she turned around to look at my mom, reached for her hand and grabbed it, and held on for a minute. Everything stopped as the ground exhaled beneath me. A big, long pause.

That same trip, Sally, who thought of my mom as a second mother, came to visit from her parents' home in Minneapolis via London where she lived with her husband and two kids. When she had asked me on the phone one day if she should visit, I hesitated. I couldn't figure out what I needed or what to say. I wanted someone to make decisions for me. I was so drained and exhausted. When she arrived, I was overwhelmed to see her and overcome with gratitude for her decisiveness and presence.

After the kids were in bed, and my mom had fallen asleep, Sal and I went outside in the backyard to lie down on lawn chairs, drink wine, look up at the nighttime sky, and cry. With chirping crickets in the background, Sally told me she felt anxious about not knowing what it would feel like to lose a parent. I thought about losing my dad and the rawness, the feeling of being swallowed whole, the waves, and the inevitable and ambivalent moving forward. But my dad's sudden death was so vastly different from what I was experiencing with my mom. I knew it sucked and also knew it would somehow be okay. Sally didn't have a reference for it.

We talked about losing people suddenly versus over time to an illness or disease, a conversation topic that seemed to come up often. I realize now that losing my mom was what I experienced when my dad died but in reverse. With my dad, he died, we were shocked, and we grieved, desperate to make sense out of something that didn't make sense. With my mom, the grieving started way before her death. Both were hard, of course, but the untimely and tragic nature of my dad's death was extremely difficult, whereas my mom had lived a beautiful life, and there was deep solace in that. But it's never enough time when we lose the people we love, and I always prayed and hoped my mom would make it to at least see eighty.

Sally wanted to be helpful and asked if there was anything she could do. There was something. My mom's cocker spaniel, Betty, had started scooting along the floor, and this could only mean one thing. It was time for Betty to get her anal glands expressed. When I told Sally she could take Betty to the vet for her expression, she laughed and said in her humorously matter-of-fact way, "Okay, dude."

As she backed out of the driveway in my mom's car with Phoebe in tow, I laughed to myself about the absurdity of the errand and then quickly was taken off guard by the deep appreciation I felt for her being there with us.

After almost two weeks in New Jersey, it was time to say goodbye to my mom and siblings again. It felt different after that visit. I didn't want to go. But I wanted to get home to Josh, and the kids were starting school soon. I cried a torrential downpour during that goodbye. I couldn't stop touching my mom's face. The tears from the corners of her eyes pierced right through me. I grabbed a pink pashmina from her closet and asked if I could borrow it.

She said, "Yes, of course," and then the kids, Sally, and I posed next to her for a photo.

We took an Uber to the airport together, crying most of the way. Sally and I held on to one another tightly. It all felt so heavy. I didn't want to say goodbye to Sally either. We laughed when

Meatloaf came on the radio singing, "I'd do anything for love, but I won't do that." Finally, after all these years, we understood that the thing Meatloaf wouldn't do was cheat on his girlfriend.

Our Uber driver dropped Sal off at her terminal first. And then the kids and I had to stand in line to get a boarding pass for Izzy because she was still a lap child with no ticket. I couldn't stop seeing my mom in my mind's eye. She looked like a child, like a baby with her round face and bald head. My heart throbbed, and my eyes were bleary. The lady behind the United counter with chocolate chip eyes and a nose ring looked at me kindly.

"I'm so sorry, I know how you feel," she said. "I haven't seen my mom in two years."

I was taken aback. "How do you know I'm sad about my mom?" I asked.

"I can just tell," she said. "I might start crying too."

I told her to take good care of herself as I walked away.

"You too," she called after me. Her empathy felt like a giant hug.

While scrolling through photos on social media, I saw a feed full of friends' and acquaintances' summer vacations with kids exploring different parts of the world. I felt guilty that my kids weren't having much fun that summer. But then I saw the words from the poem Josh hung on our closet wall: "Teach them how to cry when pets and people die." And I remembered nothing was more important than that.

Chapter 17

Medicinal Purposes

Seeing someone you love grimace in pain is an unbearable experience. That sense of helplessness, of not being able to do or say anything. There's nothing we can do.

"It's in God's hands," the nurses said.

It had been less than two years since my mom had been diagnosed with metastatic breast cancer and five months since she went on hospice. The hospice nurse knew my mother was transitioning when she appeared more confused, slept more often and deeper, and was eating less.

Fortunately, there were lots of different medications to ease the pain she was experiencing. And they were all right there at the house. On the kitchen table, in the fridge, on the counter by the phone. The thrush in her mouth, the difficulty swallowing, her bloated belly pushing on her diaphragm making it harder to breathe, the bed sore on her back, the fragile and easily torn skin—they all caused varying levels of pain. Sometimes when we asked her where she was feeling pain, she had a tough time describing how and where she felt it. She was never one to complain and had never been able to discuss easily or freely what was bothering her. When I worked at hospice as a volunteer coordinator, I often heard nurses and social workers say that people died the way they lived. For my mom, this was accurate. She was positive, hopeful, smiley, and never discussed cancer in great detail.

The in-between, the limbo between life and death, was challenging for us all.

It felt like my sun was dying. It was no coincidence that there was a solar eclipse during her last weeks on earth. I didn't bother to get the proper glasses to look at it because it was just another thing to do. And I was exhausted. I'm all about simplifying on a good day. On a bad one, it's mac and cheese with chicken nuggets without any guilt. Maybe it's laziness. Maybe it's smart. I know I'm fortunate that I know how to rest and that I actually can rest. What an absolute blessing to have an incredible support system. We all need one, scaffolding that helps hold our structures in place when the wind blows. We are not meant to do this alone. We need each other.

Part of the grief I felt then, and still feel to this day, is the loss of being someone's child. Part of getting older, and hopefully wiser for me, has meant embracing the fact that life is hard. And not because we are doing anything wrong but because it just is.

"When it rains, it pours," my mom always said.

Rain is beautiful, and life-affirming when we stop long enough to let it wash over us and let it change our plans. Life is meant to challenge us, to force us to rise to the occasion. We have no control over any of it—might as well try and go with the flow as the raindrops fall at our feet.

There is something freeing to me and helpful in accepting that life is hard. Every book I have read on Buddhism repeats this: life is suffering. But reading this and understanding it are two different things. What's not helpful is pretending it isn't difficult and messy and then filling it up with platitudes about the sun coming out tomorrow and everything happening for a reason.

I know losing my mom is the "natural" order of things. But it doesn't make it easy. I'm so grateful that she went on to lead a happy life after my dad died. I never would have thought it was possible. And as much as she missed him and missed having a companion, she spent her time traveling with friends, playing bridge, enjoying her days in her beautiful home in New Jersey, and being around her children and grandchildren. She absolutely found happiness again.

I didn't want her to die. I didn't want her in pain. I didn't want to be without her. I didn't want the awful in-between to go on forever. There was no getting better and no cure. It was a hard reality to digest.

For as long as I could remember, she had a nightly gin and tonic for "medicinal purposes."

"Are you going to have a drink with me?" she'd ask when she was visiting us.

I used to tease her that she was a bad influence. I think of what I heard recently about centenarians. All around the world, these age-defying humans take part in a daily pleasurable ritual. A cigar on the front porch. A walk. A chat with a friend. A drink at the end of the day. Every day. It's often not something we would perceive as healthy (sometimes it is), but more than anything, it's a moment free of obligations and duty, a moment dedicated to simply stepping out of all the things that have to happen and appreciating some small ritual that feels special, pleasurable, even sacred.

Sometimes when the fear and dread get to be too much, I think I need to just keep going. But then I remember that this is not really an option. Because the grief, the sadness, comes back if it's not dealt with. It manifests into something else. Anxiety, depression, an illness, a fight. If we don't take the time to acknowledge the territory of our hurting, it does not transform into something beautiful; it nests and hides in dark corners, only to come out at more inconvenient times. We must feel our feelings. We must acknowledge and express them. We must deal with our hurt and pay tribute to our sadness.

Sometimes I wonder, what if I fall into the same fate? I will want medication and perhaps even something to hasten the process. There was an episode of the Netflix show *Grace and Frankie* with Lily Tomlin and Jane Fonda where their older friend and neighbor threw a last-ever groovy party after her cancer returned and she had decided she did not want to suffer through treatment again. With lovely friends in her backyard chatting and sipping drinks, twinkly white lights and music, at the end of the night, she took a fatal dose of medication.

Back when we lived in Chatham, New Jersey, my mom took a stress reduction course with a man named Dr. Moon.

She started saying, "Let it go," all the time.

The friend she took the class with contributed a patch to the patchwork quilt her friends made her as a going-away gift when we moved from New Jersey to Scottsdale. Her patch was a red balloon floating away with the words "Let it go" stitched in pretty cursive. Dr. Moon was ahead of his time, "letting it go" long before Elsa sang the *Frozen* anthem that many of us know every word to.

As I was trying to let go of what I hoped for, of my expectations and also my fears, it helped me to focus on what I was in control of—like my perspective, attitude, how I expressed myself, whom I hung out with, and what I ate and drank. Speaking of which, I think I'll have a special beverage tonight— for medicinal purposes, of course.

Chapter 18

Labor Day

It was Labor Day weekend. When I got to my mom's house that Friday morning, she asked softly what the kids and Josh were up to for the holiday. I was amazed that she asked, that she was even aware of the date. Heather arrived later that evening. That night Kerry, Richard, Heather, and I attempted to go to my aunt and uncle's country club for dinner.

When we arrived, I knew immediately I shouldn't have come. I wanted to be home with my mom. I ordered a martini and then broke down when friends of my aunt and uncle started speaking of my mom in the past tense. My brother offered to take me home, which was exactly where I needed to be. I couldn't be around other people, only those who understood the enormity of what was going on.

Heather appeared outside the next day in a colorful, floral bathing cap and did a synchronized swimming routine in the pool while Richard, Kerry, and I sat in lounge chairs and laughed like hyenas. She looked absurd, and it was exactly the levity and ridiculousness that my siblings and I needed. My mom would have loved the outrageous performance, but she was sound asleep. I was relieved that as much as things had changed, there was still so much that hadn't. We were still ridiculous, and we were still laughing.

Family friends, Laurie and Gina, dropped off a huge bowl of bowtie pasta with pesto that Saturday evening, which we devoured while standing in the kitchen talking. My mom was sleeping just about all the time then. She said something muddled earlier that afternoon that was hard to understand. We heard, "The car is big enough." Something about "the stuff."

She said, "He's going to see about tomorrow, make sure they are all okay." Then, "It's upsetting. . ."

"What's upsetting?" I asked, and her eyes flickered. "Who is upset?" I followed up, but she didn't respond.

And then in that tender moment, Richard said, "Well, whoever it is—she will get over it."

The welcomed comic relief made Heather, Rich, Verna, and I all laugh out loud once again as we stood around my mom's bed.

I later found out while reading some hospice literature that talking about traveling is a common phenomenon among people in their last days. We were living in a cocoon in those days. I had not watched the news or picked up the phone other than to talk to Josh and the kids. Kristi called to ask me if I knew about the hurricane. I had no idea that a massive storm was brewing and Tampa was projected to get a direct hit. I turned on the news at some point and found it completely surreal to see Anderson Cooper standing in downtown Tampa. Josh and the kids flew out to New Jersey the next day while Kristi and her family of four, plus two grandmas, evacuated their house, taking our dog, Poppy, along with her two dogs and one cat to Georgia. My neighborhood was under a mandatory evacuation, and thankfully, our dear neighbors, Jody and Tif, took a video of the inside of our house in case we needed it for insurance purposes.

My mom's breathing had become labored, heavy, rattled, disturbed. It was awful to hear. It is referred to as the death rattle, which is not at all a comforting term! It made me think of the Grim Reaper with creepy chains lurking around the house. The hospice nurses assured us it was more painful for us to hear than for her to experience.

My siblings and I took frequent breaks walking around the neighborhood when we weren't by her side. We rested and read books. At one point, when I was next to my mom, my arm on hers, I quietly sang, "Glory, Glory, Hallelujah." I don't know gospel music, but my friend in grad school taught me this one, and I love to sing it. I sang it somewhat timidly and quietly while the hospice nurse sat close by. I sensed something releasing and something else rising within me and around us.

When the continuous care nurse with hospice first came, he asked us who was my mom's favorite. My sisters and I smiled and looked at Rich. The nurse told us that people often waited until the one they were closest to was either in the room or away. He told us that every time we said goodbye to her, we should make it definitive—not "See you later" but "Goodbye." He told us to make sure to tell her that we had everything under control.

We sensed that maybe she would rather die with us not in the room. I imagine that it's hard for a parent to let go in front of their children. She was fighting, holding on, and this was heartbreaking to witness. We didn't want her to die. We didn't want to say goodbye. But it so clearly felt like it was her time to go, so we said "Goodbye" and "I love you" over and over again. We told her that it was okay for her to go, that we had each other and that we would be okay.

On the third night, we told her we were going to take care of each other. We told her we loved her again. And finally, we went to bed. We left classical piano and jazz playing on the speaker in her room. There was a different nurse there that night. He was quiet, gentle, graceful, and very kind. Verna was still with us thankfully. My mom was surrounded by cards (funny ones and sweet ones), fresh flowers, and candles. Betty, the dog, still sneaking into her purse, seemed especially anxious in those days. The windows were open, and it was a beautiful late summer night.

I slept in her bedroom upstairs, and at 3:00 a.m., my phone rang. The nurse told me my mom had just taken her last breath. My sisters woke up without me telling them, and the three of us stumbled downstairs. We called Rich, and he was there five minutes later. Josh and the kids would be arriving later that evening.

In her room, the full moon shone through the skylight. The lights were low, and the music was still playing. Even after all that time, all the hours, days, and months leading up to this point, rehearsing in my mind and heart what it might feel like, we stood there in disbelief. It felt like the passing of a storm—the wild and all-consuming nature of it all: the pelting rain, the howling wind, the flashes of light, and the crashing thunder. Eventually, it all just stops and all that is left is profound stillness and silence.

I went over to her, and she looked peaceful. No more struggling, which was a huge relief to witness. I slipped the sapphire ring off her cold finger, the only piece of jewelry she still had on, and put it on mine. We broke into a million pieces as we waited for a different nurse to come over and pronounce the time of her death for the death certificate. The nurse arrived, and then the undertakers finally arrived. I almost laughed out loud when I saw their appearances. They looked like characters in a movie, dressed in long, dark coats and hats.

We said our final goodbyes. Again. It was the last time we would see her physical body. We were not in the room when they took her away. I went to the front of the house and watched from the window. It was early morning and misty out. There on the grass was a family of five deer bearing witness to her going. I felt awe, wonder, gratitude, and so much love and appreciation for those beautiful creatures in that moment. The undertakers drove off with her body. Our parents were now both gone. Even though we were adults, we felt like orphans. I went into the backyard.

Now what?

And on that strange morning—more typical of a northern California summer day than an early New Jersey September, my mom's favorite month—was a brilliant and full-spectrum rainbow. Right above her room. Heaven (or whatever is up there and out there, where we were before we were born and where we'll go when we die) was celebrating. She had arrived.

Chapter 19

All I Feel Is Love

My sisters and I left for the funeral home a couple of hours after they took my mom's body. We got into my sister Kerry's car in my mom's driveway—this place of so many homecomings and goings; of sitting in cars talking to friends or kissing boyfriends and not wanting the night to be over while seeing my mom's light still on in her bedroom; of my kids riding bikes and skateboards; of cars filling up every inch of space for impromptu gatherings or parties; of the new pink spray roses that were planted a few years ago that my mom adored.

In the distance, as I grabbed the handle of the car door to get in, remarkably and unbelievably, I heard the faint sound of bagpipes. Heather, Kerry, and I stood there awestruck and shared the same thought: my dad. My dad who lived in Scotland as a child, my dad who loved bagpipes and had a band of pipers perform at Heather's wedding and then again at his funeral. From time to time, we heard a bagpiper who lived in the area playing. That he was playing on this morning of all mornings in the middle of the week felt like a sign. It felt as if my dad was welcoming her and wanted us to know it.

We picked up Rich from his house on the way to the funeral home. We arrived and walked up the stairs into the old Victorian house in Red Bank, which felt like something straight out of the HBO show *Six Feet Under.* A recurring thought surfaced:

I can't believe everyone goes through this.

I had this same thought when my dad died and also when

I had my babies. These events that are so huge and out of the ordinary that seem to be under wraps most of the time but when they happen are so intense and otherworldly.

My siblings and I sat around a shiny wood table and talked to a pleasant enough older man dressed in a suit and tie about details like prayer cards (which we didn't want), the small service at the cemetery that would happen in a couple of days, the service a week later at the church, and the obituary. The cemetery was the same one where my Aunt Joan, my mom's parents, and my dad were all laid to rest. I thought about when I was little and we would take road trips and how my parents liked to take detours through pretty cemeteries in places like Mystic, Connecticut, and Santa Barbara while admiring the greenery, views, and shady trees. My mom would joke about how a certain spot would be a nice place to be. It drove me crazy, and it was really hard to hold my breath for that long, which was something a kid told me I had to do when going by a cemetery because it was rude to breathe in front of people who couldn't.

The man in the suit led us to the "showroom." Was it really called a showroom?

I kept correcting myself silently, *Don't say "coffin," Lindsay, these are "caskets." "Coffin" sounds like we're talking about vampires.*

But a *showroom*? A *showroom* is where you look for a car, not for your mom's forever home. I think about her navy-blue convertible in Arizona with the "Life's a Beach" bumper sticker on the back. My grandmother, Nana, never cared for the message and would say to my mom, "Susie, you are so much more positive than that."

The man in the suit told us we could take our time in the showroom. The very last thing any of us wanted to do was take our time in the coffin—I mean *casket* showroom. None of us felt like our mom cared about a fancy and expensive model. We looked like teenagers scattering around the room, giggling, feeling out of place, wanting to cry and leave and shout as we perused the merchandise. I couldn't believe how expensive they were. I wanted to get the fuck out of there.

Later that evening, while it rained heavily and we all were meandering around the house, not knowing what to do with ourselves, the side door finally opened as the bells jingled on the doorknob, and in came my kids and Josh. We never had an alarm system, just bells on doors and barking dogs. I was so relieved and grateful to see them. It had been six days since I left Tampa to be with my mom, but it felt like it had been three weeks.

Hugging Josh and the kids made my heart swell with relief. It felt like a warm blanket that I wanted to wrap myself in. We huddled together like penguins in a snowstorm, taking a moment together before having to weather the storm. It was one of those moments when time seems to stand still. Due to the impending hurricane, flights were wacky. So Josh, Will, Phoebe, and Izzy, still in diapers, had to drive to Orlando, where they boarded a flight to Cleveland, and then had a two-hour layover before finally arriving in Newark.

Once we welcomed everyone, it was back to the numb navigation of a house without my mom. We didn't know where to go, where to sit, anymore. The house that we all loved and had always brought so much comfort and joy felt so different. And empty. We sat on the couch in her room where hospice thankfully had already come and taken away the hospital bed.

I told eleven-year-old Will—really reassuring myself—that this was awful but that we would experience the awfulness together and that somehow that would make it more bearable. I told him that everyone who would be around us in the upcoming days felt exactly like we did. They all loved Susie so much and were so sad she was gone.

It helped, sharing the sadness with others. I thought of the cast of characters like our cousins (my cousin Robin coming all the way from Sweden) and friends like Sally, Kristi, Brandon, and Derek (dear friends from Semester at Sea); Kristin from San Francisco; and Erica from Maine who would fill in the raw spaces soon, and I immediately felt lighter, better, held, and so profoundly grateful for them all.

Verna was still there too, only for one more night, and then she would be leaving to go back to her apartment in New York City. None of us were ready to move on, to leave this all behind. During the next few days, I talked to my mom out loud when I was alone in the car or the shower. I told her everything. How I was feeling, what was going on, and I asked her how she was. It helped me feel close to her.

It struck me as so profoundly odd that she couldn't tell me what the experience was like for her, after all that we had just gone through together. When I was younger, my mom used to tell me that I talked to hear myself talk. I still do. But in this case, I wanted to hear her response. Will I ever know the answers to any of my questions? Are there answers? What happens when we die? Where do we go? Maybe this is something we aren't meant to know. Maybe life would suck if we knew. Maybe this not knowing is what makes life more interesting, albeit scary. But the sadness and the answerless questions burn my throat. We get through these times. Something gets us through these times.

When we think about it, we can't imagine how we could ever survive losing the loves of our lives. It is strange and beautiful to me that this grief is love, that this is love in another form. And that this love is so all-encompassing that it can't just disappear; it transforms, changes shape and matter. Energy doesn't just disappear.

I think of the time when Will was little, about age four, and we were getting out of the car after a swim lesson, and I shut his finger in the car door. He cried, and I felt awful like the worst mom in the world. How could I be so careless and reckless with this little angel boy and these tiny, fragile fingers? I gave him ice. He was fine, but I was guilt-ridden all day. Later that evening, I apologized again and asked him how he was feeling.

He said, "All I Feel Is Love."

Chapter 20

After

Taking it day by day, moment by moment, step by step was all I could do in the days after my mom's death and funeral. The hurricane thankfully spared us in Tampa, and my mom's funeral was a beautiful tribute, with lots of old and new friends and family. But it was also a bit of a blur. We spent a few more days in New Jersey before heading back home to Tampa. It was hard to leave Richard and Kerry and all the support I felt there, but thanks to my amazing friends and my in-laws, I came home to a fridge full of groceries, cooked meals, and flowers on the kitchen island, by my bed, and in the pots outside by the front door.

I learned after my dad's death that coping mechanisms, like numbing and escaping, didn't work for long. And the awful thing about numbing is that it numbs the good stuff too. I tried to find gratitude daily. Multiple times a day. I counted my blessings. I wrote down in the morning and before I went to bed at night what I was thankful for that day. Sometimes I simply paused and noticed. It was small, but the impact was big. I paid attention to the little things, and thankfulness filled up every part of my being. It's close to impossible to be anxious when you're actively feeling thankful.

Here, in the space of thankfulness, I'm in my body, out of my head, and it's peaceful. Calm in the chaos, stillness under the choppy waves. It comes and goes, but if I close my eyes, there are times I feel steady like a tree or a mountain—solid, proud, strong, rooted, grounded. I feel like everything is okay. And two things can exist at the same time, even bewilderment and joy. I am my soul. I am the sacred center.

Gratitude anchors me to this day. I'm grateful for friends, a rainy day, reading an engrossing book, a dinner out with Josh, and the orchid reblooming in the backyard. I'm grateful for my health and for the kids' and Josh's health. I'm grateful for security, safety, comfort, food, Vera's chocolate chip cookies, days without plans and obligations, naps, and when the palm fronds dance with the breeze, making the most intoxicating gentle sound. I'm grateful for medication that keeps my blood pressure, cholesterol, and anxiety in check. I love it when the jasmine in our backyard is in bloom. I'm overjoyed when I see signs like cardinals and butterflies, hearts, or feathers appearing on my path.

They help me to remember that no matter what, there is always something to be thankful for.

I keep doing for others. And taking good care of myself. This often means rest. I say no when I don't want to do something. The pausing, the checking in, the focusing on feeling the sensations in my body and neutralizing them. They aren't good or bad—they just are. Do I feel tightness, enthusiasm, constriction, or expansion? I inhale through my nose and blow out my mouth.

I won't let fear take me down. I invite trust and faith instead. I'm not going to pretend I'm okay when I'm not. I ask for help when I need it, which is often. And I don't apologize when I start crying in front of someone. I cry a lot.

I love this quote I see everywhere but don't know who said it about being the things you love most about the people who are gone. I like to be friendly and chatty when I'm out and about in the world because it makes me feel close to my mom. She was always kind to everyone everywhere and radiated light and warmth.

I want to remember what she loved too because it feels like

a way to be close to her, to enjoy what she enjoyed. Below are some of the things she loved:

- Pickles (there were no less than five to ten jars in her fridge at all times).
- White Castle hamburgers.
- New Jersey corn and tomatoes; chicken from the poultry farm in Long Branch; and sloppy joes from the Hickory Tree Deli in Chatham, New Jersey.
- The English countryside; Italy; Spring Lake, New Jersey; Nantucket, Massachusetts; New York, New York; and Carmel and Santa Barbara, California.
- Salt. (According to my mom, there was no ailment that soaking in Epsom salt couldn't cure. Gargling with salt water was always a good idea too. And sprinkling salt on food, not bad either.)
- Making up songs. (Oh boy, were there some goodies like "Chicarina Soup" or the operatic ditty she sang when feeding our gray Persian cat, Cassidy, "Oh, Casadilla.")
- Turquoise, which was the answer to the question Phoebe asked her repeatedly, "Susie, what's your favorite color?" (She also loved "shocking pink," the pink that Alida, her oldest friend who died two years before she did, also of cancer, wore.)
- Babies. (She called herself a "baby nut" and said, "You couldn't spoil them by holding them too much or letting them sleep on your chest.")
- Flowers (namely, peonies, hydrangeas, roses, and gardenia, but not gladiolas because she thought they were "funereal").
- Bridge, *Name That Tune*, and *Jeopardy*. (She was good at them all and said they were helpful for her brain and memory.)
- Music. (She loved "Claire de Lune" by Debussy, the song our friend Chaz wrote for her, and whatever my brother or my son played on the piano. She adored jazz, especially Stan Getz and Ella Fitzgerald, whom she referred to as "my Ella." She also loved Barbra Streisand, Carole King, Carly Simon, Simon & Garfunkel, James Taylor, and Harry Connick Jr.)

- The ocean (to look at, not to go into).
- The sand, the sun, and sand dollars (the beach plus friends equaled "good therapy").
- Sleeping with the windows open (because "it's good for what ails you").
- Dogs, especially golden retrievers and her late rescued black cocker spaniel, Betty. (She loved the Westminster Kennel Club Dog Show and had an impressive breadth of knowledge when it came to breeds. At the park, a cute dog would walk by with their owner, and I'd ask her, "What kind of dog was that?" She always knew. "Oh, that's a Dandie Dinmont.")
- Conversation. (Her friendly banter and genuine interest in others were both awe-inspiring and, when I was little, annoying. So was her level of detail when she repeated the story again.)
- Her fireplace in her cozy family room, my favorite place to be when it was cold out.
- Beefeater's Gin, diet tonic, and a lime. (A drink a day for "medicinal purposes.")
- Red lipstick and clip-on earrings. (Always. Even right after surgery.)
- September (her favorite month at the Jersey shore with cooler temps and drier, bluer skies).
- Bread—rye, pumpernickel, and sourdough, not wheat. (She'd say that Bonnie, her friend who was also a nurse, told her that it was okay that she chose white over wheat because contrary to popular opinion, wheat was not good for everyone— she'd say this while looking at me.)
- Paul Newman, George Clooney, and De Niro. (We don't say his first name—it's always simply De Niro. "He can park his shoes under my bed anytime," she'd say about the aforementioned men.)
- Her friends and family. (Her relationships were absolutely what got her through the toughest times.)

When I miss my mom, I drive to Woody's, a small deli here,

and get a turkey on croissant with cranberries. I eat it in my car while listening to jazz. Or I call a friend or sibling. I cuddle with Josh, my kids if they'll have me, or my dog or cat. I tell a Susie story or donate to one of her favorite charities. I do something nice for someone, and I feel her in and around me. It turns missing her into celebrating her, and that feels good.

Chapter 21

More of Something Else

When I'm sad, I don't want to be cheered up. It feels dismissive, out of touch, and frankly, annoying. I know it's more about the person doing the cheering, and that's their business, not mine.

I miss my mom's silliness. She would get that look in her eye. I miss her fits of laughter when she would watch TV or while playing a board game like Scattergories. I miss her singing ridiculous songs. And I miss her voice.

I feel distracted. Then I worry about my mental health. Is my mind okay? Am I talking on a cell phone too much? Blood pressure? Tumor? It used to be car accidents that made me worry; now it's cancer too. Gun violence. Drugs. It's always something.

I keep reminding myself that the present is the only place to be. It's more bearable than hanging out in the past and feeling down or jumping into the future and feeling anxious.

I remembered recently something I said to my yoga teacher and close friend Charlotte when my mom was first diagnosed with metastatic breast cancer:

"No one is ever going to love me like my mom loves me. No one cares about me like her. She wanted to hear the minutia of my life, what my kids ate, and how funny it was when they tried to pronounce certain words like *leave-es* instead of *leaves*, or that my youngest calls hotels 'shotels.'"

Charlotte reminded me that there are still people in my life who want to hear those stories. It's not the same, of course, but they're here. Sometimes in yoga, when Charlotte would cup my face in her palms while I lay in Savasana, it felt so maternal and nurturing it made me cry. I'm beyond thankful that love comes through multiple sources.

I have felt this at the sweetest times, like once when I got a manicure when I was feeling down. The woman massaging my hands did so with such care and tenderness that I melted into a sea of appreciation and love. The other day, while listening to a podcast with one of my favorite authors, Anne Lamott, she spoke of her fear but said that her faith was bigger. I hold on to this. I feel fear, I feel great sadness, but I am not those things, and I feel more of something else.

There is something—something unnamable, mysterious, omnipresent, benevolent, wholly kind, accepting, and loving. It's not religious because it can't be named. I believe in this. I feel it. I have always been interested in spirituality, in the sacred beat in our lives, in finding meaning. I believe in God, which to me is *love*. It feels both like everything and nothing, and it's all inexplicable, so why do I even try? Maybe that's the basis for poetry, trying to name the unnamable?

Here I am, residing in the softness in my belly, the "me-est" of me, the most authentic me. This is the biggest love there is. It's undying. It is the invisible cord that connects me to my mom and my children to me. It connects us all to one another and to every living thing. It's what I live for.

In the same podcast with Anne Lamott, she told a story about her friend telling her that when you get on a plane, it is not the time to pray—it's far too late for that; it's time for surrender and trust. And that time is now. Surrender and trust.

Maybe dying is like being pregnant and getting ready to give birth. With the exception being, of course, that you are gifted with a wonderful baby and the beginning of a life, so not exactly the same. But the similarity lies in the discomfort, the laboring, the being in two worlds at the same time, the leaving of something and entering something else unknown, the transition, the transformation.

If we're here, it means we survived birth, and birth is intense. We can get through death too, whether it's ours or someone we love. I remember telling my mom that death couldn't be that bad because no one ever came back to warn us against it.

She laughed and said, "This is true."

When pregnant, birth can sound especially terrifying, because things can go wrong. When I gave birth to my firstborn, Will, labor was progressing normally until it wasn't. I went from dancing in my family room, to laboring at the hospital in my hospital bed, to being wheeled into an operating room for an emergency C-section. It was scary and, ultimately, lifesaving.

The time comes when being pregnant is so uncomfortable with stretched skin and heartburn that you are ready to burst and you just want the baby out even though you are scared to death. But the only way out is through. You keep breathing and, eventually, pushing while relying on others for help and knowing that the rest will take care of itself. Surrender and trust.

In dying, maybe the discomfort gets bigger than your fear, and some part of you knows that death is a gift, a blessing. It rescues you with peace and the promise of the cessation of pain. The time comes to let go. Surrender and trust. Something takes over during our scariest moments—this I believe.

I recently read in a novel by Ann Patchett that safety is a story we tell ourselves. We can never really protect ourselves and our loved ones. Accidents, unfortunately, happen. No matter what.

If I could share something about aging parents, it would be this:

Have the conversations, the difficult conversations, like, *"Where do you want to live, and what is most important to you as you age?"*

There are DNRs and living wills that need to be discussed and forms to be filled out, and sooner is better than later. And something I really love is what Rabbi Steve Leder calls an ethical will, which encompasses writing down answers to questions about one's values. Questions like, "How do you want to be remembered?" and "What is most important to you?"

I know there is a greater force swirling around us, holding us, carrying us, bringing us to our knees, taking us to our limits. The very essence of this is what matters most. This deep being. Having been present with my mom before she died; having held her with my heart, hands, eyes, ears—it's a big, beautiful mystery.

My brother said it best when he said, "It's like I'm living in both worlds."

It struck me as so true. In the land of the living and that of the dying.
My sister Heather had said, "We have to keep choosing life."

Over and over again, we make the choice to come home. I saw a *Peanuts* cartoon the other day that said, "We are all going to die someday. But not today."

Choosing kindness, choosing to see through the frustration to the light—to what connects us, to what makes us whole. The realization that we are more similar than we are different, that we are all going to die, and that while we are here, we might as well try to stop complicating everything and try to find joy . . . this is what it feels like to be alive.

I think that if we spend our lives loving people, apologizing when we mess up, thanking them for being in our lives often, and forgiving others when they mess up, we are cultivating heaven on earth. This seems like the best gift of all.

Continue to stay open, open to the miracles all around you, I tell myself this daily.

The helpers, the angels, the woman whom I just let pass in front of me at the drive-through at Dunkin Donuts and who bought my coffee and munchkins and had a "Dog Lover" bumper sticker and a smile that I caught shimmering in my mirror like light on water. I am so grateful for this stranger and her kindness. I'm grateful for love pouring out from so many places. Thankfulness fills me up. Surrender and trust.

Part III

*Shame dies when stories
are told in safe places.*

– Ann Voskamp

Chapter 22

When Friendships Change

Growing up, my mom had heaps of friends. My oldest sister too. I can hear my mom saying, "Heather has so many friends." It was as if it was a badge of honor. My mom had her good, old friends (the original eleven), neighborhood friends, bridge friends, walking friends, friends from Newcomers, couple friends, parents of her kids' friends' friends, and the list goes on and on. The birthday cards that covered her mantle in her family room were like nothing I had ever seen.

After my dad died, when my mom was only fifty-three, her friendships became that much more important. She traveled with her good old friends to Europe and Florida and newer bridge friends to Palm Springs, California. She regularly spent New Year's Eve with a couple of her closest friends, and she viewed her time spent with them as therapy. I'd annoyingly correct her and tell her it wasn't the same thing. But she was right because being in fulfilling relationships is therapeutic and has a whole host of health benefits, like lowering blood pressure and expanding your life span. Her relationships with family and friends were what kept her going after my dad died.

I don't recall my mom having any breakups with friends. There were friendships that faded over time in the usual way many do, due to moves or other uncontrollable circumstances, but there were never any major upheavals that I know of.

As an adult, I have had breakups with friends, and it's been really challenging, especially knowing how essential friendships are to our overall health and happiness. There is no guidebook on the matter and a lot less discussion around breakups with friends than there is around romantic breakups. I've sought out guidance from therapists, psychics, and friends who are open about discussing their experience on the matter. I'm not sure if it feels more common today because of my age or the divisive climate of the past five years due to politics and the pandemic, but there seems to be more collective commentary about strained friendships than there used to be.

Every time one of these major shifts occurred, I first doubted myself. *Was it me? Was I overreacting? Was there something I could have done differently? What was wrong with me?*

I've learned to press pause on the self-doubt- and anxiety-inducing queries in favor of a more helpful and productive line of questioning.

I now ask myself questions like, *How do I feel after spending time with this friend? Do I feel supported, heard, appreciated? Misunderstood, confused, like I don't belong or I'm not accepted here? Do I feel like the friendship is mutual, meaning we both initiate contact and plans, or does it feel one-sided?*

The answers to these questions are often quite clear. It's feeling that something isn't particularly good for me and then having to do something about it that sucks. It's challenging and painful. We're messy humans with vastly different experiences, so it makes sense that trouble would arise in our friendships from time to time.

If you're repeatedly feeling like there is something wrong and it's not a once-in-a-blue-moon kind of argument but a more toxic, crappy, pervasive feeling with a certain friend, then what are the options for moving forward? Do you talk about it? Let the friendship fade over time? I think it totally depends on the nature of the relationship and what you want it to look like. Can you remain friends and maintain clearer boundaries for yourself? Or is that not going to suffice? Dr. Brené Brown's work on vulnerability comes to mind. Not everyone has earned the right to hear our stories. Not everyone gets unlimited access to us.

If you are consistently feeling unsupported or like you're walking on eggshells around a certain friend, this is a sign that something is awry. And that maybe he or she doesn't deserve your time, energy, and affection. If you have forgiven them for hurting your feelings in the past, but the behavior never changes, this also doesn't bode well for continuing a friendship. There are people we can talk to about what is upsetting us; they listen and make a concerted effort to understand and change. Then there are those that don't or most likely can't. Our time here is precious and fleeting; we deserve relationships that are mutually beneficial, respectful, and loving.

A friend and I stopped speaking when it became crystal clear that we had very different ways of seeing things. I'm super sensitive; she, not so much. We tried to make amends, but I felt too hurt about the things she said. She was never going to acknowledge her part in our undoing. It was time to move on.

What was eye-opening to me about this situation was that when I spoke to a mutual friend over coffee one day in the midst of the turmoil, she said, "Trust me, she is not spending anywhere near the amount of time thinking about this."

It was hurtful to hear, but I was grateful she said it. I needed to energetically let go of the bond, the attachment we had had in the past, and accept where we were now. It was up to me to accept the reality that she didn't care for the relationship in the same way I did. It was wildly painful and sent me into some daunting anxiety, but my healing had nothing to do with her. I needed time and support to take care of my own bruised heart. The kind of reconciliation I had dreamed of was simply not going to happen.

Author Elizabeth Lesser writes about erring on the side of connection. I keep this in mind always. But then there are times when it's simply not an option. Not everyone is going to meet you soul-to-soul, not because they are total a-holes—maybe some are—but more likely, because they don't have the tools to do so.

You might come to the conversation baring your whole, big, beautiful soul, wearing your emotions on your sleeve and ready to get it all out in the open, and the other person arrives cloaked in ego, feeling the need to protect and defend themselves. Understandably, we're all a bit terrified of being hurt, abandoned, and deemed unlovable. But if someone can't meet you in the same state of vulnerability, the relationship is going to suffer.

Things happen, and relationships change. It's a normal part of life. I love my friends profoundly and feel so fortunate to have such dear ones in my life. But not everyone is meant to be in our lives forever. Some friendships change and can survive things looking different, and some end.

I will no longer abandon my soul to keep the peace or to keep someone else happy. I'm committed to showing up for myself and taking care of my needs and wounds like I would if my kids were hurting. If one of my children told me someone was being mean to them or being consistently weird, I would tell them to talk to the friend to see if it's worth working on or hang out with someone who didn't treat them like crap.

Most of the time, friends aren't intentionally mean or trying to be hurtful; they are most likely doing the best they can and are just complicated and messy like the rest of us.

I'm also learning and getting more comfortable with the fact that there will be plenty of people with whom you simply skate on the surface. And that is fine—and even good—because can you imagine how exhausting it would be if every time you said hello to someone, you ended up crying and hugging and had to cancel everything because you just had a breakthrough? There are a lot of friends to be had out there and a lot more acquaintances. I've always felt like if we can't go deep and can only talk about surface shit, it's not worth my time, but I'm beginning to see that it is simply not true. Saying hi and engaging in small talk is beneficial too.

When friendships change or end altogether, it doesn't necessarily mean anyone was in the wrong or that it wasn't wonderful while it lasted. It also doesn't mean that you are bad for having to end a friendship that was no longer serving you. Detaching with kindness and compassion is always an option and remembering that these things happen. We're so far from perfect, and our relationships aren't either. We can move through and forward even if there is tension by loving ourselves first and foremost and extending well-wishes to our friends wherever we go and regardless of what happened.

If this is a loss you are dealing with, you are not alone. It's more common than you think. We don't have to get wrapped up in the drama and negativity. We can keep our peace. And an arm's length distance can be a great place to be.

Chapter 23

A Way to Be Here

When I first got into yoga, I practiced Ashtanga, a practice that follows a series of postures and lasts for ninety minutes. There is no music, just your breath and verbal cues from the teacher. The end is my favorite part because of a long Savasana, where you lie on your back on the floor, close your eyes, and rest for fifteen minutes.

When I practice yoga now, I'm more likely to do a restorative practice for anywhere from ten to thirty minutes. I stretch and breathe with all the blankets, blocks, and straps I can get my hands on. I'm not trying to prove anything to myself or others. I'm just moving in a way that feels good and nurturing.

When my mom was sick and I had a new baby at home, I did what I could to support my frazzled nervous system. One of the best things I did for myself was commit to a date with myself, my mat, and my dear friend and yoga teacher, Chartlotte, every week whether I felt like it or not. Charlotte's wealth of knowledge about nutrition and the nervous system, coupled with her soft voice, was the exact medicine I needed.

She'd pad around the room offering gentle adjustments and homemade oils and spritzes for the neck, face, and shoulders. The rose oil was my favorite. Often, while lying in Savasana, tears of gratitude rolled down my cheeks. Sometimes she'd treat us with homemade chocolate figs and truffles, and when she'd sense someone struggling to get into a posture, her thoughtful reminder was always, "Find a way to be here." And every time she said it, it was exactly what I needed to hear.

If sitting cross-legged is too much for the hips, sit on a folded-up blanket, and voilà! There is no pushing through, only relaxing into. I think of one time when I took a class from a famous yoga teacher who was known for her hardcore ab workouts and intense teaching style. She called me out for not paying attention. It was embarrassing. I got stuck wondering if I was overreacting or being too sensitive, believing it was good for me to toughen up and stay put. I mean, she was a rock star in the yoga universe with a big following! If that happened now, fifteen years later, I would get up and leave, trusting my own voice over someone else's. I'm not a tough-love kind of girl, and I don't put up with that, especially in a yoga class of all places. I like softness, tenderness, kindness, and compassion. Life is hard enough as it is.

"Finding a way to be here" is one of my favorite metaphors for life now too. It comes to me when I'm uncomfortable anywhere, not just in yoga. Whether it's on a plane during turbulence or at a party when people are arguing about politics, I silently ask myself, "Lindsay, what would help you to stay open, soft, generous, loving? What do you need in order to stay put and stay true to yourself?"

This past spring, I tore my ACL, MCL, and meniscus while I was skiing. It hurt like hell. I was on an easy green, almost to the bottom of the mountain, when a little girl crashed into me, causing me to fall like a newborn fawn. Ski patrol was on the scene quickly, and I took a toboggan ride down the hill to the clinic while trying to stay awake as I could feel myself getting close to passing out. I was in extreme pain and left that day with a brace, crutches, and a script to get an MRI once I got home. Recovery has been slow. Surgery was scheduled and then canceled as my knee wasn't ready for the procedure. Now I'm rehabbing my knee without surgery.

The woman I first worked with at physical therapy, although perfectly nice, was not all that encouraging. She pushed down on my knee so hard it only exacerbated the swelling and created more fear and apprehension in my mind. I'd come home with an inflamed knee and a deflated spirit almost every time. After a couple of weeks, another therapist told her to ease up. She mentioned to me that she had hoped my knee would be further along than it was. And when I came to therapy one day in tears, after finding out that my surgery had been canceled, I muttered, "I'm trying." Another therapist overheard and said, "Try harder." That was it. I was done. I found a gentler therapist in a quieter space who has been immensely helpful. I'm not so tense, and I can relax because I trust him. He's slow, attentive, and understands that if fear is coursing through one's body, it's going to be close to impossible to heal.

I've had to remind myself that this is not a race and that I may need something different from someone else with the same injury. It's been a very real practice in patience, going inward, slowing down, listening and honoring my body, advocating for myself, and finding a way to be here because thankfully, there is always a way.

Find a way to be here—ah yes, I think I can do that. I can pause and breathe and smile with my sensitive, silly, or sad self. Even if for a fleeting moment. I can attempt to stay present. How can we be more comfortable here? What do we need to feel secure? There is no right or wrong way. We make the rules, and harder isn't better.

Can I take a deeper and fuller breath, adjust my position, and use more blocks, bolsters, blankets, and straps? Whom or what can I turn to for more ease, help, and support? There is always a way.

Chapter 24

Writing for Medicinal Purposes

I started writing in a journal when I was seven. My first official diary, with a lock on it, of course, was a gift from a friend for my eighth birthday. It was pink and blue, decorated with glitter-filled balloons that moved around like snow in a snow globe when you shook it. I find it funny now that I had a lock on my journal then. How scandalous could the entries have been in third grade?

I had a quirky practice when I was nine, in which every other entry consisted of me writing the same exact prayer. On the off days, I'd jot down random thoughts or write about silly tiffs with friends or teachers who got on my nerves. But writing the same thing over and over again was my attempt at warding off something bad from happening. It was superstition akin to knocking on wood. Now I know it was an OCD, but then it was simply something I told myself I had to do to keep those special people safe. I never told anyone I did this because I knew it was strange and felt embarrassed about it. I talk about it freely now as an adult in the women's groups that I lead and am amazed at how common these kinds of compulsive behaviors are.

Perhaps the never-changing prayer was a compulsive habit, but writing felt cathartic to me even though I couldn't have articulated it then. Having a pen in hand and filling up blank pages from extracted emotional turmoil provided me with some relief from my anxiety like nothing else did. It did then and still does today. No one told me to write other than in fifth grade, when journaling was part of our daily English assignment. Writing was intuitive to me just as math and so many other things were not. As I child, I took ballet and jazz but stopped when I sprained my ankle in ninth grade and subsequently discovered I had more fun going out with friends.

But writing was always incorporated into what I loved doing. I made up silly songs, movies, and plays when I was a little girl. I wanted to express myself as I moved through adolescence, but it was a challenge for me to find ways to do it that didn't put me in the spotlight, which became increasingly uncomfortable for me. I never thought I was good at theater, art, or singing or that I could get better at art or music by practicing, taking classes, and also taking myself a bit more seriously. I loved to read and still do, but unlike many writers, I came to writing through writing, not through my love of reading.

I'm always in awe when I hear people say they knew they wanted to grow up and write books or that there are people who make their living writing comedic ideas for TV shows. I had no idea these careers existed!

I wrote a bit less in my teens than I did as a child, but I came back to it in my twenties, especially when I was traveling. I filled every corner of the pages of journals from Semester at Sea in my junior year in college, then later during trips to national parks, and when I spent eight weeks in Europe after graduating. My journals then were about what I did, not how I felt.

Now I write primarily about how I'm feeling. I include funny things my kids said, observations and stories I don't want to forget. But mostly, it's a way to sort through what I'm noticing, feeling, and experiencing. Over the years, I have embraced the transformative power of writing as a therapeutic tool. It's helped me get clear about what I want, and it allows me the opportunity to simplify things when they feel overly complicated. When I write, I extract meaning from my experiences. Writing is a spiritual and creative practice for me now, something I crave and try to do daily.

When someone pisses me off, the first thing I do is call my brother. He makes me feel better. Maybe he talks shit about the person that upset me like he used to when the mean girls in middle school taunted me for no reason in the food court at the mall. But if I'm really upset and there is emotional stickiness hanging around in my heart and gut, I require more time and space to process it. I'm not as adept at talking, and I sometimes stumble over words, forgetting them altogether or mispronouncing them. Writing is a more freeing and forgiving form of communication. I write letters with no intention of sending them, but I let the words spill out of me—no filter, no holding back—and it feels damn good to get them off my chest.

It's simply a way of deeply processing and validating my own feelings. If it's something I'm going to share either in a blog post or essay or with a friend, I write to release the poison first. Then I edit the heck out of it and share a more thoughtful response rather than my first reaction.

In turn, I feel more compassionate toward the person I'm writing to or about. It helps me grasp the reality, the truth of the matter, instead of turning to narratives tainted by my feelings. It often helps me to see another side and perspective. It simply shifts something and changes the energy. It's a reminder to not take things so personally and to keep softening, opening up, and reaching toward connection and understanding.

The following are other ways I use writing therapeutically:
- When I feel sad, I write free-form. I write at least one thing I'm grateful for, or I write a letter from my wise self to my sad self. (Unsurprisingly, my sad self is usually my inner child, feeling lonely and misunderstood.)
- When I feel stuck, I write about my dreams, what brings me joy, and what I would do if I could do anything I wanted. I give myself permission to dream big and have fun while doing it!
- When I feel overwhelmed, I make lists.

- When I feel anxious, I write first how I'm feeling; the more descriptive, the better. I figure out where the feeling is located and what it looks like.
- If I'm dreading going somewhere, like an event where I'm going to be with a lot of people I don't know and I'm required to mingle and make small talk, I'll write out my intentions. It helps me remember that this isn't about me, it's about the people I'm showing up for. And I don't want to shy away from things because they're hard or awkward.
- And when I'm really irritated or antsy-pantsy, what do I do? I don't write. I jump, dance, shake my arms and hands, or take a walk, and I feel instantaneously better. I've got to move with it, get it out. Sitting and stewing are not usually helpful for my brain and heart.

My mom used to tell me I talked to hear myself talk as I flitted about, talking utter nonsense a lot of the time. I still do this, but I also write to feel myself write. Self-reflection is good medicine, and it's as simple as grabbing a journal, a piece of paper, a computer, or a phone and identifying how I'm feeling and what I'm noticing without holding back.

Chapter 25

Reflective Questioning

Once my therapist told me she had never met someone with such a profound need for self-reflection. I'm not sure how to take this, but it's true. I crave time and space to process experiences and feelings. Blame it on being highly sensitive. But reflection helps me understand and love myself as well as connect me to others. Without it, I would be walking around really confused and probably depressed a lot of the time. Contemplative practices such as mindfulness, meditation, and journaling are so helpful and essential to my well-being and to the circles I lead.

Provoking questions and journal prompts are extremely beneficial especially if you aren't one to write streams of consciousness on a blank page (which I recommend too by the way). But good questions at the right time are potent medicine. Taking time to answer them honestly and spaciously shines a bright light, a clarity, and an awareness of what's most important to us.

Once, while sitting at Panera with my friend Jenny from grad school—who also happens to be a skilled Kundalini yoga teacher, life coach, and circle facilitator—she asked, "Would you be able and willing to spend the rest of your life exactly as you are, exactly as you feel right now in this moment?"

It set off a resounding internal alarm prodding me to reflect on all that was going right in my life and also what I needed to change.

When my mom's health was rapidly declining, I was home in Tampa walking my dog when a male neighbor, who was a veteran and about ten years younger than me, stopped and asked me how I was doing. It wasn't the question he asked but the way he asked it that made me tear up. And that he then cared enough to listen to my answer felt so incredibly kind and healing. It was a simple enough question, but he asked it with such sincerity and genuine empathy on such a shitty morning. He was present, engaged, and made me feel less scared and alone on that too-quiet spring morning. The connection was short, sweet, and exactly what I needed.

When a question is revealed, it steers us in the expansive direction of truth, hope, and possibility. It opens doors to more questions and more revelations.

In the circles I lead, as we sit in solidarity and support of one another, we try our best to listen fully, allowing each other the time to be heard without judgment and without offering advice. These moments often start with a brief journaling session using a prompt such as the ones below so we can sort out our thoughts and feelings before sharing them out loud.

I'm reminded too of my mom, who was always interested in other people's stories. She was interested, which made her interesting.

The questions below are not ones I made up but ones that have been asked of me by friends, coaches, authors, and teachers. I have attributed the questions that I can recall to the correct author when and where I can, but I apologize for not remembering where the majority of these questions originally came from.

If you so choose, grab your journal or pad of paper and answer the ones that speak to you or answer them over time.

Write, don't think. Feel, don't think. No one needs to see these answers unless you want them to. If you're afraid of someone reading them, burn the pages or throw them in the trash! And don't worry about a perfectly constructed response or correct spelling or grammar. Tell the inner critic to shut it. Keep moving your pen or pencil, don't stop.

(If you're interested in starting your own circles, these questions can be a great place to start!)

Know that no answer is silly, stupid, not enough, or too much. We engage with questions differently and in a more embodied fashion when we write by hand, so try to do this first if possible. If not, using a voice recorder or typing out your answers on your phone or computer is great too. And we may answer these questions differently over time, so revisiting them on occasion is also helpful. Give yourself permission to be as honest as possible with your answers.

1) Ask yourself: *What about me is unchanging? What is the thing in me that has always been there, during good and bad times? Describe what is constant.* (From meditation teacher and author of books such as *Radical Acceptance*, Tara Brach.)

2) Make a list of what brings you joy and why. Be as abstract, as simple, or as detailed as you wish. Engage the five senses when you answer this one. *"I feel joyful when I smell jasmine blooming in spring because it reminds me to breathe, relax, and take it easy."*

3) What do you believe your unique gifts and contributions are?

4) How do you serve, show up, and help others?

5) What is your personal definition of something greater? (If you believe in this.) How do you define *God, soul, spirituality, love?* (The first time I heard anyone asking these questions in this manner, it was Oprah on her show *Super Soul Sunday*.)

6) What have you always wanted to try but have come up with a million excuses not to?

7) What, if anything, would you do differently if you knew

your life would end in three years? Six months?

8) How do you want to be remembered after you are gone?

9) What do you like most about yourself?

10) Can you accept and love yourself exactly as you are in this moment for the rest of your life?

11) What can you stop doing to make room for what's most important to you?

12) How do you take care of yourself spiritually, emotionally, mentally, and physically?

13) What do you do for fun?

14) What do you remember loving as a child? What could you get lost in?

15) What did you dislike as a child?

16) Envision and describe what an ideal day/morning/birthday/holiday/vacation looks like to you. Use as much detail as possible. Who are you with? Where are you? What do you see and hear? What are you, wearing, eating? How do you feel?

17) Explain your limitations.

18) What do you need in place when feeling stressed or down? What would a survival guide look like for you? (I recommend making a survival guide anytime you go into a situation that causes you stress say hosting a holiday meal with a lot of people . . . Think of how to make it less stressful and more enjoyable and, most importantly, how you can ask for help.)

19) What kind of relationships are nourishing to you? List the people you can count on that you know are there for you in the way that *you* need. Not who should be there for you but the ones that really are. Your answers may surprise you. Also, while you're at it, what do you need? Don't be afraid to say it and share it.

20) Make a list of all the things you loved about someone you have lost. Also, make a list of what they loved.

Chapter 26

Dear...

A lot of times, I write letters to myself. I asked my teenage self what she needed to hear when I was struggling, my new mom self, and the me here today who is feeling sad about the state of the world. Try writing a letter to yourself from a place of loving concern and support. If it feels good, make it a practice.

And please note that if any of these practices I mention in this section feel too "navel-gazing" to you, they are meant to make you feel a bit uncomfortable. They are designed to help you grow and heal too. When we take responsibility to heal our wounds, we can then be there for others in real, responsible, and adjusted ways. That's always the goal.

Below is an example of me writing to my seventeen-year-old self.

Dear Lindsay,
You are safe. You are strong.
I know how scary the last few months have felt, having had your world turned upside down, first with a cross-country move and then with your dad's tragic and untimely death. When doctors talk about the biggest stressors in life, moving and experiencing the loss of loved ones are right up there in the top five. So, my love, no wonder you don't feel like yourself. No wonder you are angry, sad, and exhausted. That is to be expected.
And when you feel joyful and happy, that is okay too. So is anger, shame, embarrassment, all of it.
No need for guilt, which is a pointless load of malarky. Your dad knows you love him. Our people, when they go, want

us to keep living, loving, and enjoying life.

This loss doesn't define you, and neither do your thoughts and emotions.

But this loss will change you. Let it. You have been offered the gift of insight, perspective, empathy, and compassion. When you want to cry, let it out and cry as much as you want. Never let someone make you feel bad or silly for crying. If they ask you why you are crying or what the matter is or, worst of all, to stop crying, ignore them. Tell them crying is good for you and that maybe they should try it sometime. Anyone who tells you to stop crying has work to do. Also, you don't owe anyone an explanation.

While so much feels different, there is so much that remains the same. Look for those things when you feel particularly nervous or uncertain. Things like the sun going to bed as it slips below the horizon, the moon shining on the water, the rain falling, the blooming flowers and swaying trees, music, favorite TV shows, yummy food, your blankie, your dog Buffy, and friends and family who feel easy and comfortable to be around. Laughter. Good books. Movies. What feels warm, gentle, and cozy—go in that direction.

Sometimes you may not want to talk about what happened or how you're feeling, and that is okay too. You may want to turn it off, forget about it for a while, and that is completely understandable. Never feel like you have to get into anything and everything because someone is asking you to. You can cut it off whenever you wish or never even begin. It's up to you. You get to decide.

You can trust that very wise, competent internal guide of yours. When the world feels noisy and overwhelming, simplify. Say no, take quiet time for yourself.

And when it feels too quiet, call someone. Go have an adventure, an ice cream, or a walk.

You may want to talk to someone, and when you do, go to someone who isn't afraid to be real. Who gets it even if they haven't gone through this specifically. Someone who listens well and doesn't try to stop you from saying what's in your heart. Someone who can sit with the pain, tears, and discomfort as you retell the story of how your dad died. Someone who won't try to cover you in niceties and platitudes. Someone who isn't trying to fix it or make you feel better because this can't be fixed. If someone says there is no such thing as an accident, or everything happens for a reason, you may politely choose to say, "I don't believe that." Or give them the finger under the table.

It's not always easy to find someone who talks openly and honestly, but it's worth looking for. And if you emanate that, if you provide that for others, the right people will come to you. Vulnerability, while not comfortable, is contagious, courageous, and in turn, therapeutic.

You may need to repeat this story over and over again as you make sense of what happened.

No one is perfect. No one's life is perfect. Everyone makes mistakes. Everyone experiences loss. Life can be sad.

Life is messy. And that's what makes it interesting and even beautiful.

You will heal over time. And you will be able to wrap your head around some aspects of this. But some parts of it may leave you with unanswered questions. It will always be sad and unfair that your dad died in this way. You move with it, accept it even, which doesn't mean you ever forget it or get over it.

Know that thoughts are just thoughts. They don't mean anything! When you have terrible ones or weird ones, know it doesn't make you weird or terrible. It's just part of being a human; these thoughts come and go. We choose which ones to pay attention to. They aren't you. And they certainly don't define you. We humans are an awkward lot. When you feel like this tragedy may be a hoax, like the whole thing was a mistake and your dad is really in the witness protection program and that was him in the car next to you . . . Or you dream that this is a nightmare, and you will wake up soon to realize it's not real, it's your brain trying to make you feel better. It's totally normal. This happens to a lot of us.

Your nervous system is shot, sweetness. You've heard of "fight, flight, or freeze." It's your body's physiological response to stress. Our bodies are smartly trying to keep us from harm. Feeling jumpy, startling easily, or being shaky is also normal. You can take a deep breath and talk to yourself like, *"You've got this, I'm proud of you, you're safe, I love you."* Don't bother hanging out with people who drain or bug you. You don't need to explain yourself. Hang out with the people who love you for being you.

The people at school who stare and don't know what to say . . . It's annoying, but they aren't trying to be assholes. They most likely feel badly but are at an utter loss for what to do or say.

It's normal to be laughing one minute and crying the next. There are lots of beliefs and ideas about what happens after we die. You get to choose what makes sense to you. It doesn't need to make sense to anyone else.

You may have five great days in a row and one awful one, which makes you think you're going backward or you're really losing it. You aren't. Healing isn't linear. It zigs and zags. Feelings aren't permanent. They come and go. I promise. Hang on.

If you don't want to talk about your feelings, sing, dance, write, paint, cook how you are feeling. Scream if you want. Hit a pillow. It's important to express yourself in a way that feels helpful to you. It doesn't matter how—just get it out. You can always tear up what you write if you're afraid of someone seeing it. You might have big emotions; there is nothing wrong with that!

You are so loved. You aren't alone. You have so much to offer this world, so many unique, wonderful gifts. I know it may not feel like it now, but you will become more compassionate and empathetic because of this experience.

There are people just like you out there whom you will meet and fall in love with.

Your dad loves you. He is still here. He will continue to guide you. Stay open, soft, malleable, and in touch with what you love about him. That energy can grow, and sometimes you may even feel like you have a deeper connection with him now. How cool is that? None of the petty stuff matters. No more arguments about homework or voice lessons. He is everywhere. He is part of you. And he is and always will be around you.

If you ever feel like you want to talk to someone, like a therapist or a group of kids who have experienced similar losses, know that it exists. And this is often a good thing to try. Share your story when you feel like it.

Death is part of life. A very hard part but also what makes this life precious and sweet.

So much is out of our control. Accidents happen. It's no one's fault. It's normal to feel fear, but practice having even more faith.

You are cared for, loved, and loving. Believe you're protected. And we will get through this together. I believe you. I love you. Loving you is the easiest thing in the world. I can't wait to watch you grow and impact the world in your unique, amazing ways. I'm always here to listen when you need me. Ta-ta for now.

Love,

Me

Chapter 27

What I Know After Going Through What I Went Through (And What I'm Still Working On)

I took an online writing class during the COVID-19 pandemic, and one of the prompts was to write about what you know after going through what you went through. I immediately started making a list of what I learned during and after the experience of my parents' deaths.

Over drinks and during long night chats with friends and family, the topic of death and dying inevitably comes up. Maybe it's just me. Or my age. Or that I'm a little—some may say a lot— weird. But when it does, we tend to go down a veritable rabbit hole of speculation about the best way to die, as if there is a best way. What's worse, we contemplate: losing someone over time to an illness or suddenly in an accident?

Clearly, there are no answers to these questions. And I only can speak or write from my personal experience, having lost my dad in a car accident when I was seventeen and my mom to cancer when I was forty-one. They were two radically different situations with a variety of factors, the most significant being the way in which my dad died as well as my age and his age when it happened.

Losing my dad in a car accident made me painfully aware of how anything can happen at any time. I know I'm not in control. I don't take a minute for granted, and I don't think you should ever wait to drink the good wine, light the expensive candle, travel, or live where you are yearning to live until after you retire. Because who knows if you will ever get there. This knowing is a blessing and a curse and has certainly contributed to a fair share of my fear and anxiety. I'm nervous to begin with, and losing my dad in an untimely and tragic manner didn't help me in that department.

But the blessing is, I now have the tools to help regulate my nervous system and cope with my big and beautiful emotions. And the knowledge that my family has gone through shitty times and we're still a family and always will be no matter what. We've lost family members and gained new ones. (My sister Heather is now a grandmother.) We will always miss our parents. And be beyond grateful for our bond as siblings.

While I don't take anything for granted, which can be exhausting, I also don't take anything too seriously. I'm a big fan of slowing down and resting. My house is messy a lot of the time, and I don't let that bother me. I'd rather have people over and not worry too much about the house looking perfect. Use paper plates. It doesn't matter. I don't do perfection, and perfection doesn't keep me up at night.

Losing my dad suddenly was not only traumatic, but I was also young when it happened. If it had happened when I was an adult, it would have been terrible but I would have had (hopefully) more experience and perspective under my belt to better navigate the ups and downs.

Looking back, I think the single thing that would have been the most helpful during this time was if I had gone to therapy—be it group or individual—and stuck with it. I needed help normalizing my grief. I tried one or two sessions and gave up. Knowing what I know now, if I had stuck with it, I would have felt less alone and less anxious, and it would have helped tremendously with the PTSD symptoms that I experienced for years.

My mom's death was totally different. I was older and had my own family, and we as a family had time to sort things out, both emotionally and logistically, before she died. One of the most pressing lessons for me was, when she first got sick, my siblings and I wondered whether it was okay for her to stay in her big house alone. She did not want to leave and did not want full-time help. But that moment when it first crossed our minds was the moment to ensure more safety protocols were in place. My mom falling was the beginning of the end, and it caused her to be in the hospital for a week and then two weeks at a rehab facility. She didn't want a live-in caregiver, so it was an impossible situation to honor her wishes and do what was best to keep her safe. As hard as it is, it's never too early to talk about our priorities, values, and wishes regarding our health and end-of-life care.

I'm a big proponent of hospice care being brought in sooner rather than later because it helps ease the burden for the entire family unit, not just for the patient. Hospice is not about giving up hope; it's about making the most of the time left. It's about making the individual the most comfortable they can be in their own, familiar surroundings.

I know I sound like an advertisement for hospice care, but I know too many people who have waited until the last minute to discuss end-of-life options only to have their beloved family members spend the last weeks and days of their lives doing unnecessary medical procedures in the hospital. My mom did not want to talk about her impending death. She held on to her denial, which was very hard for me, but I had to surrender to it, knowing that this was her choice, her coping mechanism, and her life, not mine. When hospice did come in, we called them visiting nurses, not hospice, which drove me nuts, but it was what my mom wanted.

My experience has also been that most physicians aren't forthcoming in talking with their patients about palliative care and dying. I'd urge anyone and everyone to get help from experts in the field of palliative care. Research the Zen Hospice Center and doctors like author BJ Miller. Books like *Being Mortal* by Atul Gawande and *When Breath Becomes Air* by Paul Kalanthi are incredibly insightful and helpful. Know that you are not giving up; you are being realistic and trying to do what is best at a very—if not the most—challenging time.

Take a moment to write down what you think you want regarding the end of life. What are nonnegotiables for you? What is most important? It's a little like writing a birth plan: none of the things you want may actually come to fruition, but it doesn't hurt to think about and share those plans and intentions with your loved ones.

Write what you know after going through what you went through. It can be any topic at all. But it helps to see how far you have come and what you might be able to share with others about your experience. A friend of mine has three older sons and is full of good advice. I'm so appreciative that she shares what she has learned with me!

Below is a list of what I learned from losing my parents:

Healing can't happen until our nervous system has had time to regulate, calm down, and acclimate. (I will be spending the rest of my life toning and caring for my nervous system because it was way out of whack for a long time and still is on occasion. Given the fast-paced world we live in, where we know what's happening as it's happening, this is no surprise.)

It always helps to find something to smile about. Always. And not in a Pollyanna kind of way, in a real way. Something small like a flower popping up through the sidewalk, a pet sleeping in a cute position, a funny show, baby toes, the blue sky, any glimmer that gives you a moment of respite and glee or calm and deep appreciation.

Even when life is at its most awful, lighthearted moments keep us going. It's okay, and it should be encouraged to laugh during these times. Like when Heather asked the hospice nurse who came to pronounce the time of my mom's death if she was sure she was dead. It was dark, absurd, and awful and made us all laugh as we cried.

Appreciate what is working. Focus on the people who are helpful, the food that was made and brought over by friends, the ice cream that was delivered, the way the kind woman giving you a manicure gently touched your hand tenderly. Soak it up. Literally allow yourself to drink up all the kindness of these caring and thoughtful gestures. This makes it all more bearable. It is easy to look at the people who aren't reaching out, but it's so much more helpful to focus on those who are. But we have to train our brains to do this because it's not how we're wired. (Google "negativity bias.")

Losing a loved one to an illness can be excruciatingly difficult in the months leading up to their death. And you start grieving their loss long before they die, which is strange and difficult but also helpful when the time comes. Know that you aren't weird and there is nothing wrong with you. It allows you—as painful as it may be—to say "I'm sorry" or "I love you." Anticipatory grief is normal and even helpful. It's part of the process of letting go.

At the time of their death, you may feel a sliver of relief or a lot of it. You may feel a sense of thankfulness that they are free from pain. That you don't need to worry anymore. You might feel guilt for feeling that way. It's complex. But it's perfectly okay and wonderful to have feelings of ease and gratitude that the person you love is no longer suffering.

Everything is impermanent.

We're going to die.

Losing someone you love suddenly, on the contrary, is a complete shock to your entire being. There is no preparing, so it takes a lot of time and space to process the trauma and to "wrap your head around it." Give yourself all the time you need. And know that at different times of life, you will grieve the loss again. Grief comes and goes. Forever. But the rawness and the sharpest edges, I believe, soften over time.

Don't worry about the stages of grief or going backward or forward. Grief is not linear. It's also personal and different for everyone. There is no right or wrong way to do it. Give yourself permission to grieve your way, and honor what feels good to you.

It's not that time necessarily heals all wounds, but time is required to tend to them.

Breathing deeply helps regulate the nervous system and signals to our brains that we're safe enough to take deep breaths, we're still here, we're alive, and we will survive.

Candles, uplifting music, fresh flowers, something baking in the oven—they give life and make a space feel good, cozy, comforting, and colorful.

Talking out loud to our loved ones during their death keeps us feeling connected to them. It's soothing to the soul. You may not hear them respond, but you will likely feel it. I talked to my mom a lot when I was driving in my car or taking a shower; it helped me feel close to her. If there was something I had to tell her, or I was immensely missing her in a moment, speaking out loud to her provided a buffer for my extreme aloneness.

When taking a shower, let the water wash away the sorrow for a moment. Let the water drip off your fingertips, taking with it anything you don't want or need anymore. Our emotions flow like water, and swimming, a shower, a plunge, or a bath is often helpful.

Survival mode may look like bathing, walking, eating, and making sure your animals and people are fed. That's it. That may be all you do in a day, and that is enough.

A silver lining about grief, if there is one, is that everything else gets put on the back burner. It's an opportunity for real, raw truth, honesty, and clarity. It's about what really matters and who matters most. It is a sacred, beautiful, and nourishing cocoon.

The immense, all-consuming pain will not be there forever. It will subside. It will get better.

Wanting things to be different from how they are is when we suffer the most. But we tend to question, what if they or we had done things differently while our loved ones were still alive? We may relive the last months and days over and over again in an effort to make sense of what feels unimaginable.

Our relationships continue long after our loved one dies. Talk to them, and talk about them. Share stories. Say their name. Look at photos. Watch videos if that feels right. Create that feel good and right to you. It's not the same as being with them in the flesh, but it's helpful to feel them and how they still impact our lives. Notice how they still show up in our lives.

The serenity prayer is helpful to me:
God, grant me the serenity to accept the things I cannot change, the courage to change the things I can, and the wisdom to know the difference.

When in doubt, doing something for someone else helps take your mind away from your own suffering. During a period when I was having panic attacks, I painted a fence for a service project, and keeping my hands busy occupied my mind. Plus, I felt useful and productive, knowing that I helped someone else out. It's nice to know we can still be of service when we are going through our own stuff.

I always appreciated getting cards and "thinking of you" texts. It means a lot and not just in the days afterward but especially in the months and years after the death of a loved one. My sister had a friend from college who sent my mom a note every single year on the anniversary of my dad's death. It meant so much to all of us.

It's also nice to keep a piece of clothing like a sweater. I wear one of my dad's sweaters, a tan cashmere V-neck that is so worn and soft. It used to be big on me—the bigger, the better. Now it's not that big anymore, but I love that I still have it. A shawl or perfume, something to wear and put on that's close to your skin, can feel like a hug. And if this hurts more than it helps, don't bother, or you can be like my brother and keep a bag with a wig and some Chanel perfume in it—which is a tad alarming when it comes out of the closet but may also make you laugh.

Don't wait for someone to tell you what they need or wait for someone to offer help. Offer or ask for something specific: "I'm at the store, do you need milk, toilet paper, chocolate?" Just drop off the brownies, flowers, or dinner. Or "Can you please bring Johnny home from school, I need a break." Anything and something is better than nothing. And people want to help! Getting used to asking for what you need and accepting help has made a huge difference in my life. It reminds me of how interconnected we are. Support is everything, and we all rely on one another for different things.

Crying makes us feel better. There is nothing to be embarrassed about. Tears are a gift. They are meant to be released. They help us come back to homeostasis when we're stressed out. When other people react crazily to your tears, remember, it is more about them than you.

Levity, lightness, and laughter help. Don't be afraid to laugh. It is okay to feel joyful when feeling sad. It is not a betrayal to the person you lost. You can be both at the same time. Yes, and . . .

Going to therapy is usually a good idea. How to find a good therapist? Ask around, check online at *Psychology Today*, and check with your local hospice who will have a grief or bereavement center.

Getting a massage or Reiki or any other energy healing work helps release tension and feels relaxing. Unless, of course, you are someone who doesn't like to be touched. But getting back in the body, noticing sensation and feeling, is healing.

Trying to fix, give advice, or share a story about someone you knew who went through something similar (but not really at all that similar) is probably and most definitely not helpful. When others do this, remember again, it's them, not you. You don't have to pay attention. Don't take offense or take it personally. You can say thanks and think of the Instagram post of the cute dog and baby instead.

Other unhelpful things to say are, "Things happen for a reason," "There are no such things as accidents," and "God doesn't give you more than you can handle." It's like telling someone to "Calm down" or "I'm worried about you." I don't know about you, but when someone says they are worried about me, I immediately get defensive. "I'm fine, why?" Even if I'm not. It's just not a soft, welcome invitation to be vulnerable and open. It feels like an attack. No one wants that energy forced on them.

We're all awkward and weird. No one knows what they are doing. Everyone is winging it.

To show up for others, to really be present and loving, we must first show up for ourselves. We take care of our broken hearts with heaps of self-love, compassion, forgiveness, gentleness, and kindness. Again . . . and again. We speak kindly to ourselves. We laugh at ourselves, at putting our feet in our mouths. (Why does the expression sound so much stranger when you make it plural?) We take responsibility and work on our own stuff. We fill our own voids with what makes our souls truly happy (downtime, writing, nature, long walks, coffee, and cuddling our animals), or we will look to fill them with anything sparkly or distracting (and not necessarily good for us) that comes along.

Go at your own pace.

There is no shame in our faults, limitations, bad days, mishaps, and imperfections. There is so much beauty in them and often hilarity too.

When pissed, be pissed. Owning our feelings lets them move through us and not get stuck. There is nothing wrong with anger. Convincing yourself you are fine when you aren't or that you really want to go somewhere when you don't can backfire. Trust yourself. And expressing anger in healthy ways can be so cathartic. Go to a break room and throw plates, scream into a pillow, exercise, move.

Those who really love us and whom we love will not abandon us for being ourselves, owning our truths, not responding to a text right away, and/or canceling plans when we are not up for something.

Rest (not occasionally, but all the time). And this can look like watching something on TV in the middle of the day, lying down and napping, or just shutting our eyes for a bit.

Feeling connected to something outside of ourselves, to something bigger, greater, and wholly loving helps us feel less alone. It keeps things in perspective. It gives life meaning. That which is out there is also within. It's created from the same miraculous spark.

Nothing makes a ton of sense, so stop trying to figure it out.

You are not in control.

Relationships are the only things that matter. Essentially, it all boils down to love. How you love yourself and your people (your family and friends), strangers, animals, the environment—how you show them love, how you respect, nurture, and express it. Our people are everything. No need to be afraid to tell them. Tell them!

Things work out. Even if they don't.

Death isn't the end. Energy doesn't just disappear; it transforms.

We have a lot to offer.

We are all alchemists with the power to turn fear, despair, heartbreak, and struggle into something golden and helpful. Post-traumatic growth is real and amazing. But if we don't have the energy to weave that pain into magic every moment of every day—that is fine too! No pressure! Go slow. It will happen.

> We are not human beings having a spiritual experience. We're spiritual beings having a human experience. (Pierre Teilhard de Chardin)

When we feel the most cut off, disconnected, hopeless, and lost, chances are we are also cut off not only from the souls of others but also from ourselves and the source or soul of the universe. At times like this, it is easy to forget that we are all interconnected and that everything in nature is interdependent. Put your hand on your heart and belly and breathe. Give yourself a great, big hug. Nourish yourself with good food, lots of water, and something soft, sweet, and loving. Go inward.

What does your soul, your intuition, need, crave, and long for?

It's okay to take a break from your grief.

Don't go to the hardware store looking for milk. Charlotte reminds me of this often. If you keep going to the same person for validation, but they actually make you feel like shit, go to the person who is warm and makes you feel wanted, welcome, accepted, and loved. Go to where you can be you.

It's okay to not want to hang out with someone who is annoying you at the moment.

It's okay to change your mind.

We need help. Asking for help is not weakness; it is strength.

The times that were hardest were also when I felt the most supported, held, and ushered by something bigger than me—something universal, collective, loving. That gives me great solace when I feel anxious to know that something infinite, wise, and eternal will help us get through the most challenging times.

My friend Jules, who spoke at her mom's funeral, recently said, "Something came over me." She was amazing up there.

And it does—something comes over us to help us deal.

Life is meant to be tough. It is not tough because we are being punished. Because we did something wrong. It is tough regardless. And we can do tough. We are made to bend with the wind like palm trees.

It is not what we go through that has the power to strengthen, weaken, or change us in any way; it's how we respond to those things and what we do with them moving forward.

Where we're going is more important than where we've been. You can rewrite the story anytime.

To heal, we need to be present and in our body. It doesn't work (or work for long) to escape, numb, or run from our feelings. It helps to get out of our heads. What does your stomach feel like? What is your heart saying? Drop down to your feet. Plant the soles of your feet on the ground underneath you. We need to be at ease.

Feelings, which are always valid, may not always be true.

Same with thoughts. Do not believe your thoughts. You are not your thoughts; you are the one noticing them. Wacky thoughts are just that, wacky, and you can send them on their merry way.

Love yourself into healing.

We are not in control. (Did I already write that?) Of anything.

Stay open, no matter what. Especially in the hard times. But honor your boundaries. Strong back, soft heart.

Our struggles—be it illnesses, mistakes, fuckups—don't define us.

Comparison truly is the thief of joy. Decide right now to let go of jealousy. Don't engage in it. Decide not to pick it up. But it's normal too. When I feel it, I consciously work on letting it go. And sympathetic joy helps too. When something good happens to someone you love, celebrate with them, share in their joy!

Slowing down usually helps everything. So does unplugging.

Being creative is always a good idea! Dance, sing, tell stories, collage, paint, cook, garden, write!

There are many great healers that come in many different forms. They can be strangers, angels, ancestors, and animals, and they are everywhere.

Signs are real if you believe in them.

Sometimes we have to let go of the same thing over and over again and at different stages of life. Grieving my dad at eighteen is very different from grieving him now as a forty-seven-year-old woman, wife, and mother.

There is room in our hearts and in our days, in addition to the overwhelm and sorrow, to experience gratefulness, joy, infinite beauty, goodness, and love. When we allow grief and sadness their rightful place in our lives, when we allow them to be, and when we give them attention and love, we move with them and grow from them.

Every day I'm letting go, looking in, and living in love.

Acknowledgments

First and foremost, thank you for reading. It means a lot to me. Josh, I love you. Thank you for always supporting me—your exceptional listening skills, cooking, hand massages, and help with my writing all the way back to the early days when you edited every single one of my blog posts because I had zero confidence in myself and my writing. You are a dream come true, and this book would not have materialized without you.

Thank you to Will, Phoebe, and Izzy for being the absolute loves of my life. I am so deeply grateful for each one of you and for your uniqueness, wonderfulness, and ever-present love. Thank you for putting up with me always saying, "Hold on, I'm trying to finish this chapter."

Thank you, Mom, Dad, Kerry, Richard, and Heather, we are lucky, and I love you all so much.

Dick, there is no way this book would be here without you—your support, memory, interest, editing—thank you so much for all of it. I don't even know what to write to you, but I know you understand.

Thank you to the healers who have helped me heal: Lynn, Dr. Morse, Michael, Hyman, Tia, Phyllis, Elizabeth, Robert, Kathy, and Dr. Roberts.

Thank you to "Little" Jill, who feels like family and who could always make my mom laugh.

Nanny, Pops, Dave, Dawn, I love you, and thank you for always being so encouraging about my blog and writing. Nanny, your help with the kids has been out-of-this-world helpful. I wouldn't be the mom I am or have been able to finish this book without you.

To Kristi, Sally, Charlotte, Jules, The Wild Women on Beets, Ronna, Michele, Joanne, Mary Ann, Kim, Kristin, and Stephanie for being such consistent and enthusiastic encouragers of my writing.

Thank you, Erica, for helping me navigate the trickiest of waters at a really challenging time.

Thank you, Rebecca, for being a dear friend, and an amazing editor, and for the work you are doing to help the world grieve.

I love you all, and you have no idea how much your words of support have helped me to keep living and continue writing.

Special thanks to my Sacred Soul sisters and to all of you over the years who have attended a circle, come on retreat, or come to my house for a workshop, dance, costume party, or any other kind of weird-ass thing I was somehow able to talk you into. I love you all, and you make life bright, full, fun, and meaningful.

Katherine, thank you for your wonderful, amusing, right-on-target revisions. I'm forever grateful to my father-in-law for introducing me to your humorous, poignant, and fun-to-read work.

Stephanie Ong, your art has a very special place in my heart. Thank you for the gorgeous cover for this book! I'm in love with it.

To all the writers out there who have changed my life, and there are too many to list here, but I'll try: Pat Conroy, Viktor Frankl, Mark Nepo, Matt Haig, Judy Blume, Anne Frank, Glennon Doyle, Kelly Corrigan, Brené Brown, Anne Lamott,

Elizabeth Gilbert, Elizabeth Lesser, Dani Shapiro, Andrea Gibson, and Suleika Jaouad for writing honest, vulnerable, expressive, heart-opening, inspiring works of art. You've comforted and sustained me, impacting my life in the most remarkable ways, and I hope to follow in your footsteps.